NEW TESTAMENT MESSAGE

A Biblical-Theological Commentary

Wilfrid Harrington, O.P. and Donald Senior, C.P.

EDITORS

New Testament Message, Volume 2

THE WORLD
OF THE
NEW TESTAMENT

Seán Freyne

Michael Glazier, Inc.
Wilmington, Delaware

ABOUT THE AUTHOR

Seán Freyne did his post-graduate studies at the Biblical Institute, Rome, and the Institutim Judaicum, University of Tübingen. He has lectured on the New Testament and related topics at St. Patrick's College, Maynooth, Ireland, Loyola University, New Orleans, Notre Dame University, Indiana, and the University of Queensland, Australia. He is presently on the faculty of Trinity College, Dublin. His published works include: *The Twelve Disciples and Apostles; An Introduction to the Theology of the First Three Gospels; A Commentary on Mark;* and most recently, a major study entitled *Galilee from Alexander to Hadrian: A Study of Second Temple Judaism.*

Third Printing 1983

MICHAEL GLAZIER, INC., 1723 Delaware Avenue, Wilmington, Delaware 19806

Library of Congress Catalog Card Number: 79-53889
International Standard Book Number
 New Testament Message series: 0-89453-123-9
 THE WORLD OF THE NEW TESTAMENT: 0-89453-125-5

Printed in the United States of America.

Cover: Fifth Century Mosaic of Baptism of Christ

*For my Mother
and in memory of my Father*

Contents

EDITORS' PREFACE

New Testament Message is a commentary series designed to bring the best of biblical scholarship to a wide audience. Anyone who is sensitive to the mood of the church today is aware of a deep craving for the Word of God. This interest in reading and praying the scriptures is not confined to a religious elite. The desire to strengthen one's faith and to mature in prayer has brought Christians of all types and all ages to discover the beauty of the biblical message. Our age has also been heir to an avalanche of biblical scholarship. Recent archaeological finds, new manuscript evidence, and the increasing volume of specialized studies on the Bible have made possible a much more profound penetration of the biblical message. But the flood of information and its technical nature keeps much of this scholarship out of the hands of the Christian who is eager to learn but is not a specialist. *New Testament Message* is a response to this need.

The subtitle of the series is significant: "A Biblical-Theological Commentary." Each volume in the series, while drawing on up-to-date scholarship, concentrates on bringing to the fore in understandable terms the specific message of each biblical author. The essay-format (rather than a word-by-word commentary) helps the reader savor the beauty and power of the biblical message and, at the same time, understand the sensitive task of responsible biblical interpretation.

A distinctive feature of the series is the amount of space given to the "neglected" New Testament writings, such as Colossians, James, Jude, the Pastoral Letters, the Letters of Peter and John. These briefer biblical books make a significant but often overlooked contribution to the richness of the New Testament. By assigning larger than normal coverage to these books, the series hopes to give these parts of Scripture the attention they deserve.

Because *New Testament Message* is aimed at the entire English speaking world, it is a collaborative effort of international proportions. The twenty-two contributors represent biblical scholarship in North America, Britain, Ireland and Australia. Each of the contributors is a recognized expert in his or her field, has published widely, and has been chosen because of a proven ability to communicate at a popular level. And, while all of the contributors are Roman Catholic, their work is addressed to the Christian community as a whole. The New Testament is the patrimony of all Christians. It is the hope of all concerned with this series that it will bring a fuller appreciation of God's saving Word to his people.

Wilfrid Harrington, O.P.
Donald Senior, C.P.

INTRODUCTION

> And Pilate wrote an inscription and put it on the cross:
> Jesus of Nazareth, the king of the Jews . . . And it was
> written in Hebrew, Latin and Greek. (Jn 19:19f).

THE FACT that the author of the Fourth Gospel mentions these three languages in relation to the death of Jesus may well stem from his desire to suggest the universal efficaciousness of that event, yet in fact it is altogether probable that in the Palestine of Jesus' day it was necessary for official documents to be trilingual. That observation suggests the shape of this present introduction, but some further explanatory reasons for ordering the material in this way are called for. Language is the most obvious sign of the differences between people, as the Hebrew sage who penned the story of the tower of Babel (Gn 11) so shrewdly observed. Yet language itself, considered not just as a system of sounds but more importantly as a mode of interpreting reality is dependent upon deeper factors that lie at the heart of any people's self-identity. A slogan of the national movement in Ireland that eventually led to (partial) Irish independence in 1921 was, 'gan teanga gan tir', 'without language, without country'. But language is only part of the story. Without the freedom to express its distinctive character in story and song, carnival and ritual, arts and crafts, trade and commerce, there is a real danger that any people will lose its sense of identity and become absorbed by the larger political and cultural powers that control it.

The fact that three different languages were in daily use in Palestine in Jesus' day is a clear symptom of the many cross-currents at work in that society, often vying with one another for the heart and soul of the people. This phenomenon was not just true of Palestine in the first century C.E., but because of the extraordinary interest of subsequent generations in that area we are better informed about developments there. Yet everywhere the tensions between local indigenous cultures rooted in the past and the vast bureaucratic superstructure of taxation, military presence and organisation that was Rome were being felt. Rome had taken over from the older Greek monarchies, partly by accident, partly by shrewd expansionist policies of filling a political vacuum. The result was that in addition to its own particular genius Rome also found itself heir to and defender of the Greek culture that had been spread throughout the Ancient Near Eastern World ever since Alexander's conquests at the end of the fourth century B.C.E.

It was into this world that Christianity was born; this is the world of the New Testament. The first Christians were people from this world whose lives and attitudes were shaped by the concerns of the times just as we are shaped by our late twentieth century concerns about inflation and ecology, nuclear holocausts and genetic experiments, Jonestown massacres and exploration into space. And the responses were as many and varied as are ours today – even among those who professed the same ultimate vision of life. It is my conviction that a better understanding of the anxieties and hopes that shaped the lives of first century men enormously enriches the value of the New Testament as a tract for our times. It quickly emerges that, though shaped by time and circumstances there is a common search for human wholeness within a world of change, aggression and fear. Ultimately it is the ongoing quest for peace and justice despite the reality of evil and oppression in our daily lives. In this search the religious understanding of life plays a central role. It must be presumed that first century people opted for Christianity as their religion because for them at least it offered some more coherent picture of ultimate meaning and helped them to make greater sense of their everyday experiences – at the experiential if not the theoretical level.

This introduction is intended to fill in the details of that picture by focusing on the various cultural strands within the world of early Christianity, and sketch the way in which the first Christians responded to that world without ceasing to be a part of it or be shaped by it. Hopefully, it will serve as a suitable backdrop for the more detailed treatment of individual New Testament writings in the rest of this series. Unfortunately many good introductions to the world of the New Testament fail to achieve their stated purpose of bringing the modern reader closer to the world of the authors and their first readers. In my opinion the reason for this is that while drawing heavily on non-biblical sources in painting their picture, the necessary connections with the New Testament writings are not made. As a result the student never quite experiences these writings within the broader cultural and religious horizons where they are at home. Of course this difficulty is not easily overcome because there is so much of first century life that is not touched on at all or only very indirectly in the pages of the New Testament. So much lies hidden that inevitably one has to look beyond those writings in order to paint a full picture. At the same time we have to recognise that our knowledge of the ancient world would be so much less complete without the parables of Jesus or the Acts of the Apostles. Indeed, unlike so much pagan literature of the time which was written for the elitist upper class by people of literary and philosophical sophistication and is therefore limited in scope, most of the New Testament writings are directed to the masses from every level in society, and accordingly presuppose a much larger background. Consequently, my aim is not to repeat the excellent introductions that are already available and are listed for further background reading. Instead I intend to remain throughout close to the pages of the New Testament itself and for this reason actual citations are used as an introduction to each chapter. A time-chart has also been added and the interested reader is advised to study this as the information it contains is often presupposed in the pages that follow. In this way it is hoped that the reader will begin to experience the people behind the New Testament – its writers and readers – as real people in a real world whose religious answers and quests have meaning today because there is real continuity between their world and ours.

TIME CHART

Graeco-Roman History	Jewish-Christian History
	587 Babylonian Captivity of the Jews; Destruction of Jerusalem Temple.
	539 Edict of Cyrus, allowing Jews to return to Jerusalem.
	515 Rededication of the Temple.
	450 Mission of Esra, Reform of Judaism, making the law central.
333-323 Alexander the Great's conquests.	
300-200 Ptolemies, Egyptian rulers, in control of Palestine.	
299 Zenon's tour of inspection in Palestine.	
202 Rome destroys Carthage, ending 2nd. Punic War.	
198 Seleucids take over Palestine after defeating Ptolemies at Panion.	

Graeco-Roman History   **Jewish-Christian History**

190 Rome defeats Seleucids at
    Magnesium, who must pay
    large war indemnity, caus-
    ing financial straits.

169 Antiochus IV, Epiphanes,
    Seleucid King, plunders
    the Jerusalem temple.

167 Decree of Antiochus out-
    lawing the Jewish religion
    and imposing Zeus wor-
    ship at Jerusalem.

164 Rededication of temple
    after victories of Judas
    Maccabaeus.

152 Jonathan, Judas' brother,
    accepts the highpriesthood
    and Teacher of Righteous-
    ness sets up Essene com-
    munity in the desert.

146 Romans capture and sack
    Corinth.

142 Simon, Judas' second
    brother, confirmed as
    religious and saecular
    leader of Jews and gains
    tax reform from Seleucids.

134 Hasmonaean state. John
    Hyrcanus ruler until 104.
    Emergence of Pharisees
    and Sadducees.

Graeco-Roman History	Jewish-Christian History
133 Roman province of Achaia. Land reform of the Gracchi brothers causing social unrest in Italy. First slave revolt in Sicily. (Others were in 104-100 and 73-71).	
	104 Aristobulus, takes title King of the Jews.
	103-76 Alexander Jannaeus king of Jews. Execution of 800 Pharisees because of their challenge to his right to highpriesthood.
88-86 First war against Mithradates, King of Pontus in Asia. Subsequent one, 74-63, causes the rise of military men to power: Pompey in the East and Caesar in the West.	
	76-67 Alexandra his wife as Queen regent. Pharisees begin to play an important role in political life.
64 Pompey, Roman general, annexes Syria and establishes Roman province there.	

Graeco-Roman History	Jewish-Christian History
	63 Pompey takes over Jerusalem, dismantles Jewish state and makes Hyrcanus II high priest and ethnarch. Emergence of first Herodian, Antipater, as minister of state.
59 First Roman Triumvirate, Pompey, Caesar and Crassus.	
54 Defeat of Crassus by Parthians at Carrhae.	
48 Caesar defeats Pompey at battle of Pharsalus, Dictator of Roman world.	
	47 Herod the Great in Galilee as governor at 18 years of age, incurs wrath of Jewish Sanhedrin.
44 Murder of Caesar by Brutus and Cassius. Second Triumvirate of Antony, Octavian and Lepidus.	
42 Battle of Philippi, defeat of Brutus and Cassius.	
	40-37 Antigonus, a Hasmonaean with support of Parthians, declares himself King of the Jews. Herod given same title by Roman Senate. Eventually reconquers Palestine, and purges Hasmonaean nobles.

Graeco-Roman History	Jewish-Christian History
31 Battle of Actium, Octavian victorious over Antony and Cleopatra. Sole ruler (Princeps) of Roman world in 27, Augustus in 22, Pontifex Maximus in 12 and Pater Patriae in 2 B.C.E.	
	26 Herod's building project at Jerusalem temple.
	6(?) Birth of Jesus.
	4 Death of Herod the Great. Riots in Palestine.
	4-6 C.E. Archelaus Tetrarch of Judaea. After 6 it becomes a Roman Procuratorship. Revolt of Judas the Galilean with his Fourth Philosophy, over Roman Census. Beginnings of Zealotism.
	4-39 Antipas Tetrarch of Galilee.
	4-37 Philip Tetrarch in northern Transjordan.
14 C.E. Death of Augustus.	
14-37 Tiberius as Emperor.	
	27(30) Crucifixion of Jesus.
37-41 Gaius Caligula as Emperor wished to have his statue erected in Jerusalem temple. Crisis averted by his death.	

Graeco-Roman History	**Jewish-Christian History**
	41-44 Herod Agrippa, Herod the Great's grandson and friend of Caligula, King of the Jews. Murder of James the Apostle. Trouble between Jews and non-Jews in Alexandria.
41-54 Claudius Emperor. Expelled Jews and Christians from Rome in 49.	
	44 All of Palestine under direct Roman rule.
	51-52 Paul at Corinth on second missionary journey.
	52-60 Felix governor of Palestine. *Sicarii* on the rise in Judaea.
	54 Herod Agrippa II, son of Agrippa I, King in the territory of his uncle Philip. Retains some control over the selection of high priest.
54-68 Nero Emperor, Fire of Rome in 64 for which Christians are made scapegoats. Probable martyrdom of Peter and Paul.	
	60-62 Porcius Festus governor. Paul sent to Rome for trial.

Graeco-Roman History	Jewish-Christian History
	66-70 First Jewish revolt with cessation of loyal sacrifices and burning of Roman archives.
	70 Destruction of the Temple by Titus.
	73 Mass suicide of remaining Jewish freedom fighters at Masada. Destruction of Qumran. Beginnings of School of Johanan ben Zakkai at Jamnia.
79-81 Titus Emperor.	
81-96 Domitian Emperor.	
	85(c) Gamaliel II, head of Jewish School at Jamnia.
	94 Persecution of Christians mentioned in *Apocalypse*.
96-98 Nerva Emperor.	
98-117 Trajan Emperor. Pliny governor of Bithynia writes to him about Christians in his province in 112.	
	110 Martyrdom of Ignatius of Antioch, Christian Bishop, at Rome.
	112 Revolt of Jews in Egypt.
117-138 Hadrian Emperor.	
	133-5 Revolt of Bar Kochba in Palestine. Jewish school moves to Usha in Galilee.

1. The Greek Inheritance

1. THE GREEK INHERITANCE

In those days, as the numbers of the disciples grew, the ones who spoke Greek complained that their widows were being neglected in the daily distribution of food, as compared with the widows of those who spoke Hebrew (Ac 6:1).

Not long after this the king sent an Athenian senator to force the Jews to abandon the customs of their ancestors and to live no longer by the laws of God; also to profane the temple in Jerusalem and dedicate it to Olympian Zeus, and that on Mt. Gerizim to Zeus the hospitable (2 Macc 6:1-2).

Three kings of Persia are yet to come: and a fourth shall acquire the greatest riches of all. Strengthened by his riches, he shall rouse all the kingdom of Greece. But a powerful king shall appear and rule with great might, doing as he pleases (Dn 11:2-3).

When the crowds saw what Paul had done, they cried out in Lycaonian, "Gods have come to us in the form of men!" They named Barnabas Zeus; Paul they called Hermes, since he was the spokesman (Ac 14:11-12).

(At Athens) Epicurean and Stoic Philosophers disputed
with him . . . (At the Areopagus Paul said) . . . I discovered
an altar inscribed,'To the unknown God'. Now what you
worship in ignorance I intend to make known to you.
For the God who made the world and all that is in it, the
Lord of heaven and earth, does not dwell in sanctuaries
made by human hands . . . From one stock he made
every nation of mankind (Ac 17:22-26).

The Jews demand signs and the Greeks seek wisdom,
but we preach Christ crucified – a stumbling block to the
Jews and a folly to the gentiles; but for those who are
called, Jew and Greek, the power of God and the wisdom
of God (1 Cor 1:22-24).

BY THE FIRST century C.E. Rome was the political ruler
of the Mediterranean world, and consequently we could
easily overlook the Greek influences that were still alive
and active. One of Rome's own poets declared that 'captured
Greece conquered the arms of her captors', meaning that
though politically dominated, Greek culture continued
to shape the ethos and world of Rome. The passages from
late Old Testament books and from *Acts of the Apostles*
just cited suggest that the Jewish/Christian relationships
with the Greek spirit varied from hostility to dialogue,
and in this chapter we shall attempt to trace some of the
reasons for this changing situation.

   Mention of the Greek world naturally brings to mind
classical Athenian life and culture that has given such a
lasting legacy to mankind and which Christianity has done
so much to foster; the philosophy of Plato and Aristotle,
the dramas of Aeschylus, Sophocles, Euripides and Aris-
tophanes, the older epics of Homer. However, the Greek
world that was to contribute enormously to the development
of Christianity was of a different character to that classical
highpoint that was Athens. It is usually designated 'hellenistic' and its beginnings are associated with the conquests

of Alexander the Great of Macedon, 'the powerful king of great might who does as he pleases', mentioned by Daniel. Alexander himself did not live long to enjoy the fruits of his great conquests that took him from his barren homeland in northern Greece to the Indus river in the space of ten short years (333 – 323 B.C.E). Yet those conquests had set in motion cultural trends that could not be reversed despite the splintering of his empire among various generals and the bitter rivalries that marked the relationships between them – the Ptolemies in Egypt, the Seleucids in Asia, the Antigonids in Macedonia. After centuries of struggle in which the political empire of Alexander was never re-united, each kingdom fell in turn to Rome – Macedonia in 146 B.C.E., Syria in 64 B.C.E. and finally Egypt in 30 B.C.E. By that time however, a very distinctive culture had emerged all over the East – a curious blend of Greek and Oriental – and it was into this world that Christianity was born. Without the emergence of the larger civilisation it is indeed doubtful if it could have succeeded. We will look at some of its more outstanding features in turn.

I. The Hellenistic City

The *polis* or city-state was a product of the Greek way of life that reached its peak in 4th century B.C.E. Athens. It has shaped our political language as well as our institutions ever since. In classical times each city-state was autonomous, a self-contained unit of free citizens, having its own territory as a supporting hinterland and ruled over by a council of the citizens, at the head of which was the chief, an elected official. Though democratic, that is, ruled by the people, in name, there were other inhabitants of the city who did not share all the rights and privileges of the citizen – usually foreigners, freedmen, slaves. Obviously, such a free institution would not suit the imperial designs of Alexander or his followers, but they were shrewd enough to recognise its value for controlling vast territories of ethnically diverse peoples and cultures, and the constitution was adapted accordingly to suit the purposes of the various monarchies. Thus, we find the emergence of city-states all over the Near East as old cities were transformed and new ones founded, and suitable rewards were given to those who inhabited them as guarantors of peace and the disseminators of the Greek way of life.

Alexander himself had shown the way with the foundation of the new city of Alexandria in Egypt. Antioch was founded by an early Seleucid king as the capital of his kingdom, and both cities were to play a very important part in the development of Christianity for centuries. Gradually the east was dotted with similar foundations, each serving as a nucleus for a distinctive way of life. They were inhabited by people who were grateful for the honours bestowed on them and who were ready to do the will of the monarch in appreciation for receiving their own plot of land or the right to collect the taxes for a territory, or merely to act as a royal official – policing, collecting custom duties, inspecting and the like. At first these inhabitants were Greek veterans from the various campaigns who could be depended upon, but gradually as the native aristocracies of the various territories became more familiar with the Greek way of life, they too became part of the vast network of officials to be found everywhere in the Near East, and inter-marriage between natives and foreigners was actively encouraged.

Inevitably, the rise of the cities brought about a major shift in population patterns. Everywhere people were on the move, leaving the stability of the village and clan for the new and challenging environment of the cities. This was partly due to economic necessity as the small peasant found himself squeezed out of existence by competition from the large landowners and the exorbitant taxes that everywhere were being demanded to support bureaucracy. But it was also the result of the spirit of the age – the search for novelty and the broadening of horizons. The cities were not equally kind to all the natives, needless to say, since not all received citizenship. Yet the drift appears to have been inevitable, a fact that is strikingly illustrated by the many Jews who left the homeland in search of better economic or religious conditions abroad. Only two centuries earlier an exiled psalmist had lamented the fact that they could not sing a song of Yahweh in foreign Babylon (Ps 137), and now people were freely leaving without any scruple in regard to the ancestral faith that had tied them to the cherished homeland. The fact that the Hebrew Scriptures had to be translated into Greek about the year 300 B.C.E. in Egypt, shows how rapidly the movement abroad took place. And it is little surprise that three centuries later Paul on his missionary journeys could visit large Jewish colonies in the major cities – Rome, Corinth, Antioch, Ephesus, Philippi, Thessalonica. In Palestine also there was a marked trend towards urbanisation as city-states sprang up along the major highways or on the coast and older oriental cities were transformed with an influx of foreigners – Tyre and Sidon, Ptolemais (Acco), Gaza, Samaria, Scythopolis (Beth Shean), Philadelphia. The trend continued in Roman and Herodian times – Caesarea, The Dekapolis, Tiberias. Even Jerusalem itself, the holy city, was not immune from the changing times, and as early as 170 B.C.E. some hellenised Jews had sought to turn it too into a Greek city – only to arouse the passions of more loyal countrymen, as we shall see.

It would be a mistake to think of these cities as being the replica of classical Athens. They were not. Many of the Greeks who inhabited them were culturally not very aware, and so not very likely to bring about wholesale change of attitudes among the natives. Indeed the evidence suggests that in many cases the opposite was the case, as Greeks, isolated from their homeland, adapted themselves to the local customs, and within a few generations a new type had emerged – Greek in externals but still retaining many of the old ways of the East. More than anything else the cities provided a network of communication on a scale not previously known in the whole region. Greek increasingly became the universal language of commerce; trade-routes were opened up between east and west and people moved freely from one region to another. It is impossible to exaggerate the importance of this network of communications for the rise and spread of Christianity. *Acts of the Apostles* documents the journeys of Paul, as he criss-crossed the Mediterranean world on sea and land with the good news about Christ, but he was only one of a large number of such early Christian missionaries who vied with rival religious preachers and philosophers for the allegiance of the masses in the market places of the cities. Any contemporary missionary will testify to the value of knowing the language and being able to share many of the assumptions about life with his audience. This was the luxury that was granted the first messengers of the gospel because such a one-world culture existed through the network of cities.

II. The Economic and Social Influences

The author of the first book of Maccabees tells us that certain elements of the Jewish community at Jerusalem in the mid-second century B.C.E. felt that separation from the larger world for religious reasons had deprived them of great financial possibilities (1 Macc 1:11). These people were the Jewish aristocracy who had had most contact with Hellenism in its various forms and saw the possibilities for economic prosperity that the new civilisation had to offer. These possibilities were certainly significant. Alexander's campaigns had opened up new trade routes never before explored and the riches of the East began to flow westward in the succeeding centuries – minerals (gold, silver, copper, iron), frankincense (for religious worship), foodstuffs (corn, wine, oil, fish), textiles (especially linen) and luxury goods of all kinds. There was increased productivity everywhere due to better techniques in agriculture, viticulture, mining and the like, and the fact that money was rapidly replacing the barter system as the medium of exchange made it possible to transport a variety of goods much greater distances and to seek out more lucrative markets.

The new wealth was mainly concentrated in trade and commerce, therefore. Everywhere one finds the emergence of a wealthy middle class who were able to profit in some way from the new possibilities. Merchants are to be found in all the great cities – Antioch, Rhodes, Ephesus, Corinth, Delos (the centre of the slave trade), Alexandria and Tyre, and there seems to have been no lack of markets for their wares. Once Rome began to push eastward in the Mediterranean after 200 B.C.E. the demand was even greater, even if some of the western provinces such as Spain, and later Gaul and Britain, also supplied some of the raw materials. There was also an increasing demand for artisans, builders, people engaged in manufacturing, arts and crafts, and they too were to be part of the ever-growing, influential middle class that was to challenge the aristocracy's supremacy everywhere. Even among the Jews, the Saducean priestly aristocracy that had ruled the temple-state of Judaea since Persian times, had to make way for the Pharisees, who, Josephus tells us, were particularly popular with the townspeople (i.e. the new middle class), even in matters pertaining to temple worship. Though differences of religious point of view were operative, as we shall see, there were also very definite social implications in this shift in the balance of power, even in a religious community. In Rome itself, a new and powerful middle class, the equites or knights, emerged, originating mainly in the professional military, as their name suggests. They were to increase in power in the Empire, as the old senatorial aristocracy was purged or died out. Tacitus calls them 'new men', mainly from the provinces, whose industry and wealth did not make them any more cultivated or acceptable. Yet their control of the sources of wealth was in the end more important than social status.

While the towns were bursting with a new vitality, the countryside still remained the backbone of all hellenistic economies. However, this did not necessarily mean that the lot of the country people improved because of the introduction of better and more efficient farming techniques. The reason was that the various hellenistic monarchies adopted the policy that 'land conquered by the sword belongs to the conqueror', and so was at their disposal to lease, sell or grant as a gift to trusted friends or newly established colonies of veterans. Naturally there was a great displacement of the small landowners of earlier times. While policies varied from one kingdom to another and from one period to another, it can be said that the general trend was from free-hold peasants to tenants and share-croppers. Naturally, the ravages of war, the threat of enslavement, the inability to meet the various demands of an inequitable system of taxation affected the helpless peasant more than most, and made his links with the land tenuous at best. One particularly dreaded hazard was the billeting of armies during the winter season since this made serious extra demands on local resources that could not be avoided. Inevitably the slide into brigandage was easy and frequent and we meet highway robbers everywhere in the countryside of the ancient world, eking out an existence by attacking the trading and other caravans away from the more protected areas.

Josephus, the Jewish historian, graphically fills in for us details of this general picture in regard to the Palestinian countryside of the first century. Herod the Great, planted some Babylonian Jews in the region of Trachonitis and Batanaea (northern Transjordan), giving them special tax incentives in the hope of easing the problem of highway robbery in that region. On another occasion he had to import Egyptian grain and grant a remission of taxes because of the failure of the crops. When the Emperor Gaius Caligula (37 – 41 C.E.) sought to have his statue erected in the temple in Jerusalem, the Jewish peasants staged an agricultural strike, refusing to till the land, and the Roman governor in charge of the affair, Petronius, knew that this would give rise to a harvest of banditry due to their inability to pay the taxes. The Jerusalem aristocratic high priests sent their servants to the threshing barns of Judaea to collect their share of the harvest (the tithes) and force was actually used to collect them, leaving the lesser country priests to starve. Little wonder then that when the Jewish revolutionaries from the Judaean countryside entered Jerusalem at the outbreak of the Jewish revolt (66 C.E.), one of their first acts of defiance was to destroy the record office where debts had been registered. In the same revolt the country people of Gischala in Upper Galilee, having been embroiled in the conflict through the intrigues of one of their townsmen, John, a classic if rare entrepreneur, sought peace with Rome because it was harvest time.

This picture of conditions in rural Palestine is clearly reflected in the gospels also, especially the parables of Jesus, where the Galilean social situation comes directly into view. We hear of absentee landlords and tenant revolts (Mt 21:31-45); small family-run farms (Mt 21:28-30; Lk 15:25-28); debts and debtors (Mt 18:25-35); extortion and corruption (Lk 16:1-9); uncaring rich (Lk 12:18) and starving beggars (Lk 16:20); day labourers paid mere subsistence wages (Mt 20:1-6). What is interesting about this whole picture is that the middle class, so frequently encountered in the towns, never intrudes itself. The one exception to this in Galilee may have been the fish trade (cf. Mk 1:16-20) since Josephus tells us that the lake was populated with every kind of fish, even a rare Egyptian species. This may well have been due to a definite stocking policy of the Ptolemies when they ruled Palestine two centuries earlier. We know that they ran a monopoly on the fish trade in Egypt and it was probably as a result of similar policies in Galilee that the lake-side town of Magdala got its Greek name, Tarichaea, (literally 'salted fish'), since the process of salting made it possible to export fish even as far as Rome.

Similarly the land policies of Galilee in Jesus' day had their undisturbed roots in Ptolemaic land policy. The succeeding regimes merely administered what they found when they took over since the overall situation was so unfavourable to the ruling class. We have detailed information on this situation by some of those extraordinary archaeological finds that have so enormously benefitted the study of the Bible and its lands in our century. In the 1920's the archives of one Zenon, an agent of the chief administrative officer of the Ptolemies, Apollonius, were discovered intact in Egypt, among them a number of letters and other documents pertaining to life in Palestine. In 259 B.C.E. Zenon had made a tour of inspection of royal lands in Palestine, including Galilee and reported to his superior on the situation. Subsequently he remained in touch with some people in Palestine and his correspondence with these has also been preserved. Two pieces of information are of particular interest. Some years after Zenon's visit another agent, Glaukias, reports that he visited the village of Beth Anath (location in Galilee uncertain) and found that the estate manager Melas (note the Greek names) had done an excellent job of meeting the tenants' complaints by having a proper well sunk and by providing sufficient accommodation. As a result the vineyards were thriving and it was impossible to distinguish the local wine from the best Greek brands. While the agent is quite satisfied with what he finds and the steward is doing a good job, one wonders what the peasants had to say whose figs had failed the previous year because of lack of water and who had some of their crop confiscated to pay their rents.

The second piece of information is less enthusiastic. Zenon had written to a friend to collect some debts from a native village owner, Jaddua. The friend gives a rather lame excuse for not carrying out the mission himself, sending a servant instead. Jaddua not only refused to pay but had the servant and his retinue thrown out of the village, reminiscent of Jesus' story about the wicked tenants who maltreated the servants of the owner and killed his son (Mk 12:1-10).

The Zenon papyri introduce us to two other aspects of the economic and social scene in Palestine that were the direct influence of the hellenistic age and were to continue to be important issues for Christians of the first centuries – namely taxation and slavery. Of course it was with Roman policies that Christians were directly involved in these matters, but here again it is important to be aware that Rome was heir to attitudes and the administrator of systems that had been developed in earlier times.

We can begin with slavery, since it is frequently assumed that Christianity had its earliest and greatest appeal for the destitute classes of the Roman Empire. That some early Christians were slaves is obvious from the pages of the New Testament, especially the letters of Paul, and this must have created real tensions, since Paul repeatedly affirmed that with the new age of Christianity all human distinctions between people, even that of slave and free, are no longer operative. Yet he encouraged the Corinthians to remain in whatever state one happened to be (1 Cor 7:21). Elsewhere in Paul's letters we find repeated exhortations to slaves to be obedient and faithful to their masters, but equally for masters to be fair and generous to their slaves (Eph 6:5-9; Col 3:22-4:1). This suggests that Christian communities were made up both of slaves and their masters. It is interesting that in the gospels Jesus is never portrayed as condemning slavery directly either as a social or legal institution, even though the Old Testament had already recognised the anomaly that there were any Hebrew slaves: 'since you yourselves were once slaves in Egypt' (Dt 15:15; cf. Job 31:15). In his parables and other sayings Jesus accepts slavery without demur (Mt 8:9; 10:24; 24:45-51;

25:14-30) and indeed draws on the master/slave relationship to describe his own relationship to God and the disciples'relationship to him (Mt 10:24f; 20:24; Jn 13:13-17; cf. Phil 2:7). Undoubtedly Jesus' usage and understanding was determined by the Old Testament figure of 'the servant of Yahweh', rather than by the Graeco-Roman institution of slavery. As described in Isaiah (chs. 40-55) this figure is based on the semitic background of a high royal official, but the Greek notion of slave did not have any royal honourific overtones. Perhaps, the fact that the Christian self-understanding was expressed in such terms blunted the critique that could have been expected of the institution's dehumanising aspects when Christianity came face to face with its worst excesses. Instead, the tendency was that of spiritualising the notion rather than attacking its underlying social assumptions. In the Epistles such terms as 'redeem' and 'ransom', used to describe the work of Christ and the condition of the Christian certainly reflect the world of slavery, but they are charged with a whole new level of meaning in the light of the Christian proclamation that it is God's love that has brought about our salvation, and that this is the only matter of importance.

Though slavery is a fact of life from the earliest human records, the hellenistic age saw a tremendous increase to the point where as many as 10,000 slaves changed hands in one day at the slave market of Delos. It is not unusual to hear of wealthy Romans in the first century having as many as 2,000 slaves. This means that the conditions of slavery varied enormously from region to region and from regime to regime. Yet despite such variations the underlying reality was that of a large alienated segment of the society at the greater centres, often far away from their homelands and a potential threat to stability, either by instigating full-scale revolts as in second century B.C.E. Sicily or first century C.E. Rome, or alternatively as disseminators of new ideas such as the Stoic philosopher Epictetus from Hierapolis who came to prominence in Nero's Rome. One's fate as a slave varied considerably, depending on whether one was born into slavery as a member of an extended family or was captured through war, brigandage or piracy. The former often rose to positions of great influence in Imperial Rome, whereas the awful condition of slave labour in the mines, often the lot of those captured, was notorious even in the ancient world. While manumission, that is, being declared a freedman with certain social restrictions, became an increasing possibility in imperial times (i.e. at the end of first century C.E. and thereafter), the condition of the slave was scarcely more than tolerable. In the Zenon papyri we hear of some female slaves whom Zenon had purchased escaping to their former owner, and this causes little surprise in the light of the information from the same documents concerning the use of such slaves for prostitution at frontier posts like Gaza, on the main highway to Egypt. In *Acts of the Apostles* we read of a slave girl at Philippi who was a great source of income for her masters as a fortune teller (Ac 16:16). Paul's letter to Philemon concerning Onesimus, the runaway slave who had converted to Christianity, shows that this continued to be one possibility for gaining one's freedom, provided one was not branded, of course.

Religion was obviously an important factor in the slave's acceptance of his lot. There are no traces of a separate slave religion, and it would be incorrect to think of Christianity in that role. As noted, slaves could be the bearers of new ideas, including religion, from the homeland, and Tacitus tells us of an edict under Tiberius that ordered the expulsion of 4,000 slaves and freedmen tainted with Egyptian and Jewish superstitions. The obvious implication is that their masters could also be influenced by their ideas. Often, no doubt, the influence was in the opposite direction – a slave adopted the religion of the master, either because he had no alternative within the household where the *paterfamilias* acted as the sole arbiter of affairs, or freely, but in the hope of winning approval and eventual liberation. Nor should we forget that oppressed groups often try to emulate their social superiors. It is not unusual therefore, to find Christian slaves within Caesar's household sending greetings to their brothers at Philippi (Phil 4:22). This suggests a considerable degree of religious liberty even for slaves, and must obviously explain some of the appeal of the various cults for them; in the religious gatherings they were able to experience the freedom of association of which they were deprived in everyday life. At the same time religion does not seem to have had a significant impact in softening the institution of slavery. Christianity, we saw, did not always affirm at the practical level its theological insight that there is 'neither slave nor free', though the Jewish writer from Alexandria, Philo says that the Essenes, a Jewish ascetical group we shall meet later, denounced the owners of slaves 'for annulling the statute of nature', that all men are equal. More enlightened voices at Rome like Pliny and Seneca recognised the problem, the latter affirming that 'we maltreat slaves, not as if they were men, but as if they were beasts of burden'. Gradually however, influential Christian writers like Clement and Origen at Alexandria condemned slavery. Elsewhere, with rare exceptions, the Christian attitude was that of calling for improvement of the conditions of slaves rather than the abolition of the institution. Obviously, the tension between ideal and practice was just as real in the earliest centuries of Christianity as it is today.

The second general feature of the hellenistic economic scene of particular interest is the taxation system, since this had undergone far-reaching changes as a result of the economic and commercial developments in the wake of Alexander's conquests. Taxes and tax-collectors play quite an important role in the New Testament. Jesus was born, according to Luke, as the whole world was being enrolled (Lk 2:1) that is, being enlisted for taxation purposes, and the same evangelist tells us that refusal to pay taxes to the Romans was one of the false accusations brought against him at his trial (Lk 23:2), even though

all gospels report his enigmatic response to those who
wanted to trap him: 'Render to Caesar what is Caesar's,
and to God what is God's' (Mk 12:17). According to Matthew, Jesus was under surveillance by the temple officials
to see if he and his disciples paid the temple tax (Mt 17:24-
27), and Peter was able to reassure him that they did. These
two episodes highlight the problem for most Jews, and for
those Christians who remained close to Judaism – namely,
being subject to two tax-systems, one saecular, the other
religious, with neither taking any account of the other.
One can understand why tax-collectors were even more
unpopular in Palestine than in other societies, ancient
or modern. However, to understand the real extent of
feelings it is necessary to examine the broad outlines of
ancient tax structures more closely.

The early hellenistic monarchies farmed out the taxes of
particular areas or countries to certain individuals who were
responsible for the amount of the tribute that had been
levied on the area in question. That such a position was
extremely lucrative can be seen from a story in Josephus
which tells of the keen bidding that went on for the rights
to gather the taxes of Palestine. Eventually, one Joseph,
an aristocratic Jewish nobleman won the day, and he was
not above using armed force against some of the towns that
were slow in meeting their obligations. Naturally such a
system caused great bitterness, since the native who engaged
in tax collecting was regarded not just as a financial oppres-
sor, but also as a collaborationist with the enemy. The
tribute in question could be based on a land tax or a poll
or head tax, or both, so that nobody was likely to escape
the net.

While St. Luke paints a tranquil picture of everybody
going to be enrolled, 'each to his own city', Josephus tells
us that about the same time in the newly formed province
of Judaea some Jewish nationalists instigated a revolt
against the census for the obvious reason that being subject
to taxation was equivalent to accepting the yoke of the

foreigner. Subsequently, refusal to sow the crops (and the resulting inability to pay the taxes) or the refusal to pay the annual tribute were intended as direct acts of defiance against the Roman control of Palestine. In Roman times the taxes of the various provinces were farmed out to societies of publicans, and their harassment and extortion are notorious. Occasionally Rome did not intervene directly but simply used the 'client' king, that is the native ruler whom she sometimes allowed to stay in power, as the tax-collector on her behalf. The Herods of Judaea, Herod the Great, his sons, Archelaus, Antipas and Philip, his grandson Agrippa I and great-grandson Agrippa II, are excellent examples of this 'tolerance'. However, this meant no alleviation of the tax demands, as such individuals, whose position was totally dependent on the will of Rome, outdid themselves in levying extra money to support various military campaigns of their patrons or to contribute to vast building enterprises. Herod the Great is one outstanding case in point. Not only did he levy huge sums of money as an ambitious young man to support various Roman contenders for power, but as king he embarked on a vast building programme, the remains of which are still visible for any tourist in the Near East today. Apart from the temple in Jerusalem, there were the new cities of Caesarea on the coast and Samaria as well as fortresses dotted all over the countryside. His benevolence even extended to places beyond his realm in the best hellenistic tradition: temples at Beirut, Rhodes and Athens. The financing of such endowments had to come eventually from his own hard-pressed subjects. Little wonder there were bitter complaints to Rome after his death.

Another aspect of the general tax system of New Testament times that has its roots in the earlier period is the variety of customs and toll fees, traces of which are to be found everywhere. As already mentioned, the trading opportunities had increased considerably. This meant that a whole range of goods could be moved greater distances and customs fees had to be paid as they were transported from one territory to another. Again the Zenon papyri fill in the picture for us. With their state monopolies we meet all kinds of bureaucratic officials, especially at the ports, and naturally also we hear of attempts to pay them off or evade their all-seeing eyes altogether. In all probability these positions too were farmed out to the highest bidder since they afforded the opportunity for considerable gains over and above what was owed to the state. Inscriptions found in Palestine from the early hellenistic period suggest that such controls were in effect even between local villages, and this must have deprived small peasants of whatever incentive they might have had to produce more and bring it to the local markets. Levi, also called Matthew, who joined the permanent retinue of Jesus' followers was in all probability such a local official in the Caphernaum area (Mk 2:13-17; Mt 9:9-13) and Zachaeus, whose house Jesus visited near Jericho, was a similar official of a slightly higher rank (Lk 19:1-2). Thus, this vast network of officials continued into Roman times. The fact that Zachaeus, on meeting Jesus felt bound to declare his uprightness and his care to make restitution if he had defrauded any man, suggests that he was the exception to the rule among his kind, and John the Baptist's stern warning to the tax-collectors, 'defraud no man of anything' (Lk 3:12-13), is more typical. Little wonder then that the Jesus movement which seemed to harbour such people – tax-collectors and prostitutes – was looked at with some disdain by the religious authorities.

As already mentioned, the Jews were in a particularly unfavourable position in regard to taxes because of the sacred obligation their religion imposed upon them to provide for their temple and its priesthood. Many of the other great temples of antiquity possessed their own lands that were officially recognised as exempt from taxes. Not so the Jews, since the land that belonged to their temple was Palestine itself, the holy land, and as previously indicated it had already to meet a heavy tax burden from its overlords, hellenistic and Roman. Some concessions were made. In 47 B.C.E. for example, Caesar demanded a 25% tax on produce to be paid every second year, and the sabbatical (every seventh) year was entirely exempt. The question put to Jesus about paying money taxes to Caesar, indicates that in his day at least there was a poll or head tax to be paid also by all the adult population. Since Josephus records Caesar's decree as an example from the past of Roman benevolence to his people, it presumably represented an improvement on the previous period under Pompey and his successor Gabinius, who had conquered Palestine for Rome and parceled out the country in various sub-divisions for taxes and other administrative purposes. In effect this decree of Caesar was merely a reenactment of a much earlier one (though with changed terms) whereby certain concessions were allowed to Jews living in Judaea because of their support for the Seleucids against the Ptolemies when the former annexed Palestine in 198 B.C.E. The right of Jews everywhere to bring their offerings to Jerusalem was also recognised and we know that many from the Diaspora were most fastidious in doing so, to the point where the temple treasury, a kind of sacred bank, was the repeated target of armies invading Jerusalem. Naturally, such concessions to their religious beliefs were not particularly acceptable to local governors and municipalities, who did not want to see the money leaving their territories. The earliest roots of anti-Jewish feelings in the Graeco-Roman world lie here, for at once the distinctiveness of the Jew was affirmed with unwelcome economic repercussions, and the local temples and deities were thought to be slighted. When eventually the temple was destroyed in the year 70 C.E. the conquering Emperor Vespasian insisted that the annual half-shekel offering which every adult male Jew was expected to pay, would now go to the support of the Capitoline

Jupiter in Rome. In Jewish eyes this was the final ignominy.

Payment of taxes was not merely an economic or political fact of life but had definite religious overtones as the question put to Jesus, 'Is it lawful to pay tribute to Caesar or not?', indicates. Little wonder then that non-payment of taxes to Rome became one focal point of the Jewish revolt. Inevitably, Christians, seen by Roman authorities as a Jewish sect, became suspect on such issues also. Paul writes to the Roman Christians exhorting them to respect civil authority which comes from God and concludes:

> You must obey, then, not only to escape punishment but also for conscience' sake. You pay taxes for the same reason, magistrates being God's ministers who devote themselves to his service with unremitting care. Pay each one his dues: taxes to whom taxes are due: toll to whom toll is due (Rm 13:5-7).

Clearly this is a rather forced argument, but as an official spokesman, Paul felt it necessary to go on the record that Christians are good and loyal citizens. One detects a similar concern in Luke's writings, as by the end of the first century Christians have separated themselves more and more from their Jewish roots and do not wish to be identified with them or their alleged attitudes to the civil government of Rome. This brief look at some aspects of the economic and social situation in the Graeco-Roman world helps to introduce us more concretely to the world of Jesus, his first followers and the early Christians. They came from many different social strands in that society, ranging from the slave Onesimus to Joanna the wife of Herod's steward Chusa. Presumably they did not shed entirely the influences of their various backgrounds as they embraced the new faith which preached that all are one in Christ. It will come as no surprise to find that the practical application of that theological vision was as difficult in the first century as it is today.

III. Religion

When the people of Ephesus named Barnabas Zeus and Paul Hermes, they were betraying the kind of lively religious imagination that was characteristic of hellenistic man. Likewise, when Paul comments on the proliferation of altars in Athens, yet also points to the one dedicated 'To the unknown God', he was underlining the religious dilemma of the times. In the same Athens four hundred years earlier, Socrates had been forced to drink the hemlock because 'he corrupted the youth', forcing his contemporaries to think about the gods and challenging their simplistic notions based on the ancient myths. Shortly after Alexander's conquests, Epicurus had been even more scornful of traditional religion – in the words of his Roman follower, Lucretius, he was the one Greek who dared to invade with his mind the realm of the gods, 'til underfoot is tamed religion trod, and by his victory man ascends to god'. Even a fourth century Hebrew sage whose musings have found their way into the Bible (*Qoheleth*; Greek *Ecclesiastes*) seems to have been affected by the tenor of the times: 'Vanity of vanities, says the preacher. All is vanity'. However, such scepticism about religion did not survive very long in the hellenistic world, if it was ever shared by the common man; and long before the first century C.E. a number of developments in the sphere of religion had been taking place – all of which might be seen to be 'preparation for the gospel', if one were disposed to read history like the later Christian historian Eusebius as especially planned and directed by God for his own wise ends.

Early Greek religion saw the gods not as the embodiment of uncanny powers in nature, but as forces of moderation and purpose. Zeus is the avenger of evil; his consort Themis is the queen of lawgiving; Apollo is the god of order and equity; Athene the goddess of subtle intellect; Aphrodite the goddess of beauty and grace; Hermes the god of the favourable moment and its use; Dionysus the god of abundance and fertility. Though inhabiting Mt. Olympus and infinitely separated from man, the gods are really the patrons of human social institutions and the virtues that are required from the good citizen. Thus ideally there was an unbreakable bond between citizenship and religious practice, and the city-state was not of human but divine origin, with the gods the guardians of its constitution. However, even before the rise of Alexander and the adaptation of the city-state for imperial purposes, its sacral character had been coming under increasing attack from a number of sources. For one thing the myths, or stories about the gods' dealing with men, had begun to lose their conviction and many passages in the great dramatists suggest increasing doubts about real knowledge of the gods. Furthermore, the need to update or change the city's laws weakened the conviction that the constitution was indeed divine. Above all there was the 'rationalism' of the philosophers, based on Socrates' 'know thyself', which turned attention to human reason as the central task of man's enquiry into the meaning of life. Clearly, in such a climate the old religion could scarcely survive. It certainly could not be convincingly 'exported' to the east, which had its own ancient traditions about the deity and its dealings with the world. Indeed it does not seem to have survived at Athens itself, since Paul was to find an endless proliferation of altars there, and more significantly still, one dedicated to the unknown god.

(i) FATE, ASTROLOGY, MAGIC

Perhaps the first effect of the break up of the old religions was the depersonalising of the idea of god into the abstract notion of Tyche or Fortune. Originally this idea expressed no more than the common conviction, based on observation, that everybody's life is subject to forces and events outside and beyond their control and comprehension. Soon however, Tyche, feminine in form but impersonal in her dealings, began to replace the idea of the gods as the controllers of man's fortunes. Indeed each had his own fortune, now favourable, now unkindly, and there seemed no way to determine or control her workings. It only took a little contact with Babylonian speculation about the stars and planets with their movements according to fixed laws – a science to which Greek mathematics was able to bring added precision – for this notion of Fortune, capricious but not altogether unfriendly, to degenerate into blind Fate, hostile, unfathomable and unconquerable. It was presumed that events on earth including people's lives were determined wholly by the movements of the stars, and hence it became one of the primary tasks of religion to deal with this force – to foretell its happenings by astrology; how, if at all, it was possible to escape from it; what to do in the face of it. Thus in one piece of astrological advice from Egypt we hear that when 'Mars appears in triangulation with Mercury and Saturn, this brings good fortune and makes for great achievements'. This development gave a universal or cosmological direction to thinking about the gods, something that was also facilitated by the new political and cultural world that was emerging under Alexander and his successors. It is not coincidence to discover a correspondence between religious beliefs and political and cultural patterns. One's ultimate view of the world is shaped by and itself shapes the everyday world of space and time. We shall have occasion to return to this point later.

Matthew tells us that wise men (magi) from the East came to worship the new-born babe of Bethlehem (2:1-2), and this may be based on a planetary occurrence at the time. More probably it reflects an implicit acceptance by early Christians of current ideas that all human life was under the control of the stars and that the birth of great men in particular was marked by special astral phenomena. Yet, either as Fortune or Fate, the notion of an impersonal force that utterly determines man's situation is not consonant with the Hebrew God who calls man to freely enter a covenant relationship with him. Both Jesus and the early Christians shared this conception also.

This understanding explains the appeal of Christianity to people of all classes in the Graeco-Roman world, as we shall see in greater detail later. In the Christian view, one was no longer subject to such a power. Writing to the gentile Christians at Rome Paul was able to reassure them that 'they have not received the spirit of bondage again to fear', but the spirit of adoption. And John was able to reassure his readers that the Truth (which is Jesus) would make them free. About the same time Seneca the Roman philosopher was attempting to present as stiff an upper lip as possible:

> Fate guides us, and it was settled at the first hour of birth what length of time remains for each . . . Therefore everything should be endured with fortitude, since things do not, as we suppose, simply happen – they all come. Why therefore do we chafe? Why complain? For this we were born. Let nature deal with matter, which is her own, as she pleases; let us be cheerful and brave in face of everything, reflecting that it is none of our own that perishes. What then is the part of the good man? To offer himself to fate . . . . One unchangeable course bears along the affairs of men and gods alike. Although the great Creator and ruler of the universe himself wrote the decrees of fate, yet he follows them.

One can readily recognise the attraction of Christian liberty rather than the gloomy fatalism of the philosopher.

Indirectly, however, this blending of Greek Tyche with Eastern Astrology has left a very deep imprint on the pages of the New Testament, namely, in the presence everywhere of the belief that man is under constant threat from malevolent spirits who can attack humans, causing them all kinds of bodily and physical harm. This development is most clearly documented in the Jewish and Christian writings, but it was a general feature of the religious spirit of the times in the hellenistic age. Apparently it had originated during the Persian period in the Iranian religion of Zoroaster in which not one but two supreme beings – one good, the other evil – were thought to be engaged in the struggle for control of the world. Now Fate, considered as a hostile force, manifested her power through such spirits, and one important task of religion was to offer man some possibility of freeing himself from her clutches. These conceptions were shared by rich and poor, learned and unsophisticated alike, so that it is not surprising to find various ways of dealing with the problem – magic, soothsaying, sorcery, necromancy and the like. They all share in the belief that by the use of a set object, formula or action it is possible to compel the deity to act in a desired way. Religion can easily become debased into superstition in such circumstances and there is plenty of scope for fraud and exploitation of the unwary. The charge of being a magician or engaged in sorcery was one very effective way to discredit an enemy and put an end to his career. In the gospels (Mk 3:22-32; Mt 12:22-30) Jesus was accused of being in league with Beelzebul, the prince of demons, and Herod Antipas thought that he had conjured up the spirit of the beheaded John the Baptist (Mk 6:16; cf. 8:28). A second century C.E. writer, Celsus, accused Jesus of having gone to Egypt (the home of magic) to learn magical spells and returning with these tattooed on his body. Simon Magus sought to buy their powers of healing from Peter and John at Samaria (Ac 8:9-24). At Ephesus, the home of the goddess Artemis, whom all venerated, it is no contradiction to find many, even Jews, practising magic and possessing books on the topic presumably containing various spells and techniques (Ac 19:13-19). And we meet a Jewish magician, Bar-Jesus, posing as a prophet in the court of Sergius Paulus, the governor of Cyprus (Ac 13:6-10).

That such a consciously monotheistic religion as Judaism could tolerate magic might seem surprising, and we could easily dismiss these episodes as uncharacteristic and due to alien influences in the Diaspora. However, two centuries earlier in the militantly nationalistic army of Judah the Maccabee, fighting for faith and fatherland, we find a similar phenomenon. When some soldiers of his army fell in battle fighting Gorgias, the governor of Jamnia, they were found wearing amulets of the god of Jamnia under their cloaks (2 Macc 12:40), something that the Jewish law had strictly forbidden (Dt 7:25). Clearly human fear knows no religious boundaries, and in an age in which the dividing lines between national and cultural identities were being seriously challenged it is not surprising to find similar mingling of religious loyalties also. Nowhere was such mingling more in evidence than in the world of magic. Reading any of the many magical papyri that have survived from Egypt one gets the impression of a mumbo-jumbo of names, including that of Yahweh, the God of the Jews, and others quite unintelligible, all being invoked as part of the magical charm to ward off evil or obtain some favour. Obviously nothing can be left to chance and every possible source of help should be invoked, since Fate is such a universal, yet impersonal force, that all are likely to encounter. It is not surprising then to find the name of Jesus also being invoked by Jewish exorcists as part of a magical rite, as at Ephesus (Ac 19:13) and possibly already in his own lifetime (Mk 9:38-40). Nor is it any wonder that many opponents of early Christianity, like Celsus already mentioned, should have wanted to brand Jesus as a magician, and a deceptive one at that. If it was natural for the magician to call on all possible divine names, irrespective of one's own religious tradition, it was also very common to attribute supernatural powers to great figures, in a world obsessed with the idea of Fate, and it was a matter of one's allegiance in determining the source of that power – the Deity or the Evil One. Thus, the Roman Emperor Vespasian (70-81 C.E.) was said to have the power of healing, and Solomon the Jewish king became a legend not just for his wisdom but for his magic also. Besides, there were travelling religious missionaries claiming to be endowed with special powers and vieing for the popularity of the masses. Many of the early Christian missionaries must have been scarcely distinguishable in their appearance and approach from those of other groups, and as we shall see, this posed some serious theological as well as organisational problems for the early church.

In a word, the first impact of the Greek influence on the New Testament world was to create an atmosphere of universal anxiety and fear in the face of the impersonal force that dominated mens' lives, namely Fate. This created a situation in which the search for ways of coping religiously with life was very active, even when it often gave rise to practices and beliefs that could only be described as superstitious and bizarre. In the end, astrology, magic, sorcery and the like did not solve the problem of Fate, but merely offered possibilities of escaping its clutches.

(ii) THE APPEAL OF PHILOSOPHY

Another feature of the hellenistic religious scene was the emergence of a number of philosophical systems which to some degree took on the role that religion had previously played in the city-state. Paul encountered the Stoics and Epicureans at Athens, but there were also the Cynics and the Pythagoreans. A common feature of all these was the fact that they were not just systems of abstract thought for the few, but rather propagated for the many a way of life and a set of attitudes based on a particular understanding of the universe that each had developed. The very terminology of the various systems reflects the religions that they replaced, and in some cases incorporated. As already mentioned, the city as an autonomous institution had suffered a loss of status in hellenistic times, and this was reflected in the demise of the local deity. Instead the whole world was now to be conceived as one huge city-state,

according to Zeno, the founder of the Stoics, and consequently the search was for some kind of universal principle
that could correspond with the new cosmic awareness that
had emerged.

Of course by New Testament times all these systems had
themselves gone through a considerable amount of change
and adaptation; and in Roman times one can speak of
philosophical as well as religious eclecticism, where elements
from different systems are blended into a personal syn-
thesis, as for example with Cicero, who did so much to
introduce Greek philosophical ideas to Rome. It should
also be borne in mind that even when people did not actually
belong to one or other of the philosophical schools in
question, they were often deeply touched by their ideas
and even viewed their lives in the light of these systems.
A similar contemporary phenomenon would be the way in
which the personalist language of existentialism – for example, terms like authenticity, anxiety, world – has
become part of everyday speech in our times, even by those
who have no idea of its origins or technical derivation. It
is totally predictable therefore to find some of these 'rational
ideas' even in Judaism, with its strong revelational character. Thus Qoheleth (3rd century B.C.E.) recommends
'it is well for a man to eat and drink and enjoy all the fruits
of his labour under the sun, during the limited days of the
life God gives him' – advice that sounds rather similar to
Epicurus' 'eat, drink and be merry', as we shall see. And a
century and a half later the conservative Jerusalem scribe,
Jesus ben Sirach, was to describe wisdom, later in the same
chapter to be identified with the Jewish law, in terms
reminiscent of the Stoic speculation about the world-soul
or Logos that is found in all things (24:5-8.22). Clearly the
philosophical jargon and the ideas that went with it had
a wide currency long before Christianity, and it is worthwhile
examining briefly the principal systems, if only to see the
kind of questions they sought to answer and their possibilities for adaptation to the Christian message.

It is no coincidence that the founder of Stoicism, Zeno, was a younger contemporary of Alexander the Great, for his system could be seen to be the philosophical underpinning for Alexander's political and cultural dreams. Despite these 'propagandist' concerns Stoicism still raised and attempted to answer questions that had been alive in Greek philosophy for some time, namely, the relation of man to the universe as a whole and the relation between a man's inner and outer self (body and spirit). The answers they worked out to both questions were based on their view of the universe as an ordered and closed system, at the centre of which is the Eternal Principle or Logos (Reason), whose spark exists in all reality, man included, thereby constituting the unity of all creation. Following from this cosmology (i.e. doctrine of the cosmos or world) the first task of man is to live in harmony with the universal law of nature that assigns to each its place according to the particle of the divine reason it has received. Thus, ideally, the whole human family is but one, sharing in the same divine Logos and inhabiting the one great city-state, the *oikumenē*, and differences of race, sex, class, ability, are of no consequence. Of course at this point Stoicism was faced with the obvious contradiction between fact and ideal, and its adherents were faced with the objection that if man's task is simply to find his place in the predetermined universe then how is he really free.

In dealing with these two objections the Stoics answer to the second question posed above, namely the relationship between a man's inner and outer self, becomes crucial. That answer was simple and followed logically from their system. Since it is the divine spark that constitutes man, his inner self is his true self. Everything else that he possesses, even his body is really of no importance. Thus man achieves happiness when he withdraws into his inner self and obtains freedom from all external things. It is at this level that all men are equal, 'for you are a principal work, a fragment of God himself', as Epictetus, a Roman Stoic of the age of Nero, was to write. One is forcibly reminded of a similar dilemma in the letters of Paul. Repeatedly he asserts that there is neither Jew nor Greek, slave nor free, male nor female, but that all are one in Christ (Rm 10:12; Gal 3:28; 1 Cor 12:13; Col 3:11) yet slavery, for example, is accepted as a fact of life. Thus he advises Philemon to receive back his runaway slave Onesimus, whom Paul had converted, and to know him both as a man and 'in the Lord'.

This concentration on the true self also helped the Stoics overcome the objection about freedom in their system. In cultivating the inner self a man has to ignore all external attractions, and freedom is achieved through the increasing abandonment of the desire for such things. Nothing external is good or evil, only indifferent. The only true good is that which promotes inner freedom and achieves harmony between the self and the divine Reason that is at the heart of everything. 'How can we call him free when he has not learned to give up desire and fear?', asks Epictetus, and Cleanthes, an early Stoic, calls on god (Zeus) to lead him to the goal ordained for him, and he will follow freely, even though he recognises that in any event he would be compelled to do so. Thus the Stoics developed a sense of duty or conscience, that is, being true to one's inner self and following the call of god, and this became the cornerstone of their ethical system. On the one hand a man was called to be part of the great human family, and on the other he was invited into the recesses of his own being, there to discover true freedom from the external demands of the world. While this latter ideal of inner tranquility could have led in the direction of monasticism, or flight from the world, in fact Roman pragmatism had no difficulty in combining both aspects. The classic example is the second century Emperor Marcus Aurelius for whom social and political involvement is the way to achieve 'the unity of Nature', once they are approached in the spirit of inner freedom.

Stoicism could be described as a religious philosophy. The reason or Logos that is the heart of the universe can be variously described as Zeus, Providence, Destiny, Universal

Law, Nature. This created a climate in which monotheism, or belief in one god, the hallmark of both Judaism and Christianity, is more readily acceptable. Cleanthes (331 – 232 B.C.E.) demonstrates this tendency in his famous hymn to Zeus, which has many similarities with a Hebrew psalm to Yahweh:

> Thou, O Zeus, art praised above all gods: many are
>   thy names and thine is all power for ever.
> The beginning of the world was from thee: and with
>   law thou rulest over all things.
> Unto thee may all flesh speak, for we are thy offspring.
> Therefore will I raise a hymn to thee; and will ever
>   sing of thy power.,

Many indeed were the names of god in the hellenistic world. Local deities, with their own cult-centres were transplanted with the movement of peoples and took on universal features that tended to obscure the differences between them. In the east the head of the Greek Pantheon, Zeus, could be assimilated with Baal Shamēn, Lord of the Heavens. Originally he was a god of vegetation, especially among the Phoenicians of Tyre and Sidon, who came to acquire universal features in hellenistic times. With its religious and universalist outlook Stoicism as a way of life could easily blend with such developments, and it is not surprising to find that Christianity also borrowed much from their ethical reflections, especially their idea about a natural law. As we shall see in chapter three the Pharisaic teaching about the universal scope of the law suggests some affinities with Stoicism also, and it may not just have been a piece of propaganda when the Jewish historian Josephus compares the two movements.

On the other hand Epicureanism, the other major philosophical system that emerged in early hellenistic times and continued to have an impact later was thought to be atheistic, and opposed to religion. However, this is an overstatement, since Epicurus did believe in the existence of the gods, but considered that they had achieved such perfect bliss in another realm that they ignored humans altogether. Thus the links between the deity and man were totally severed and it was up to each individual to achieve his own happiness here on earth, since death marked the end of human life. 'So death, the most terrifying of ills, is nothing to us, since so long as we exist, death is not with us, but when death comes, then we do not exist', Epicurus bravely reasons, with more than an echo of Paul's 'Death where is your victory? Death where is your sting?' (1 Cor 15:55). It is this aspect of their doctrine that may have prompted Josephus to liken them to the Sadducees in Judaism 'who deny that there is any resurrection' (Mk 12:18). However, the notion of happiness espoused by the Epicureans was far from the popular conception based on their 'eat, drink and be merry' attitude, which apparently was open to misunderstanding even in Epicurus' own day and later (cf. 1 Cor 15:32). For he explains: 'When we maintain that pleasure is the end we do not mean the pleasures of profligates and those that consist in sensuality . . . For it is not continuous drinkings and revellings, nor the satisfaction of lusts nor the enjoyment of fish or other luxuries of the wealthy table, which produce a pleasant life, but sober reasoning and the searching out of motives for all choice and avoidance'. The Epicurean ideal could be stated in one phrase as 'freedom from disturbance' *ataraxia* – whereby a man achieved inner harmony and happiness, and virtue was an important way of achieving this goal, not an end in itself.

Epicureanism was a very different kind of response to that of the Stoics in regard to the new world order that had emerged. Its ideal ultimately led to a passive attitude in which the individual's own happiness rather than the world-state was the primary objective. Yet for those who espoused it in its pure form it was effective in helping them to cope with the political and social uncertainties of the age. It represented one option that man has always regarded as viable in the face of intractable human concerns, namely withdrawal, and as such could be seen as the forerunner of monasticism, both Jewish and Christian, without the religious apocalypticism of the former, of course. As such, Epicureanism was never very popular in the ancient world, and in Rome tended to be lumped together with other minority religious 'brotherhoods' such as Christians and Jews, as being anti-social and even subversive. The linking with certain forms of early Christianity may have been more than accidental, for Paul, in some of his letters at least, seems to be addressing a situation that would be thoroughly familiar to a first century Epicurean. Thus, for example, in the first Epistle to the Thessalonians he advises the Christian community to: 'Make it a point of honour to remain at peace and attend to your own affairs. Work with your hands as we directed you to do, so that you will give good example to outsiders and want for nothing' (1 Thess 4:9-11). Whether Paul is here addressing an actual situation that had developed at Thessalonica or is attempting to stave off in advance some possible anti-social attitudes that could be a temptation for Christians there, the fact is that both the language and the ideal of peace have definite resonances of Epicurean attitudes, which sometimes went so far as to avoid manual labour entirely: 'for then one is least entangled in business, the source of so many annoyances'.

Space does not permit any detailed discussion of other popular philosophical systems of the period, such as Cynicism and Pythagoreanism, both of which revived in Roman times, espousing moral attitudes and ascetical practices for their followers. Suffice it to say that the mere fact that these travelling missionaries are to be met every-where in the Mediterranean world in the first century of the common era is a clear indication of the tenor of the age. It is no coincidence that all these systems were practical rather than speculative in their orientation. Despite the corruption, cruelty and exploitation of the times there was a genuine religious and moral quest, and Christianity had already a very definite agenda to address, if it was to be a successful competitor for the minds and hearts of men.

(iii) THE MYSTERY RELIGIONS

There is one other feature of the hellenistic religious scene that deserves mention because of its possible bearing on Christian origins at a later period. This is the popularity of the so-called mystery religions, some of whose appeal was based on their meeting the desire for a personal God that many felt was lacking in the state or official religions. And whereas philosophy suggested ways of coping with fate, these mysteries offered the possibility of overcoming it. Originally the Greek word 'mystery' in the plural form meant religious rites in general, but gradually it came to be used of secret rites practised by a particular group of devotees, celebrating one or other of the salvation myths that arose in response to the religious needs of the times. In classical Greece, Eleusis, a town ten miles northeast of Athens was the home of the most famous of the mysteries, which celebrated the goddess of vegetation, Demeter, and the recovery of her daughter Proserpine for part of the year, from Pluto, the god of the underworld, who, according to the legend, had raped her and taken her captive. In hellenistic times, however, the mysteries were no longer confined to particular places, but were to be found in the wake of a mobile population – merchants, military personnel, slaves. Eventually they found their way to Rome, where they posed a serious threat to the old religion of the state and were viewed with suspicion if not downright hostility by the authorities. Tacitus, the first century C.E. Roman historian, speaking of the persecution of Christians by Nero in 66 C.E. rather ruefully comments that 'all things hideous and shameful (including Christianity) find their centre and become popular' at Rome. It may be that Tacitus had not taken the trouble to distinguish between these various oriental rites which for him were all symptomatic of provincial decadence invading Rome. On the other hand, perhaps there were very definite similarities, at least for the outside observer, despite the essential differences to which we shall address ourselves in a later chapter.

With one notable exception to be discussed in Chapter Three, the early hellenistic period, like the Persian one that preceded it, was a time of great religious tolerance. Thus Greeks who settled in the East were not compelled to adopt oriental customs in religion or anything else, though the advantage of their doing so was not lost on the ruling monarchies, especially in Egypt. It was probably at Alexandria, that the first conscious attempt was made to blend the older Egyptian myths with a Greek form and the result was the emergence of the cult of Serapis, which was to travel far from its originating point in the course of a few centuries. It is interesting to note how the blend effected a new creation, that was neither oriental nor Greek. According to the myth, Serapis was the incarnation of the older Egyptian god Osiris, the Lord of life and civilisation, who had become assimilated with Zeus, the father of all. Osiris had been murdered, but through the services of his sister/consort Isis and her son Horos (sun) he had become god of the underworld and of renewed life. According to a later version of the ritual, initiation was possible for laymen as well as priests, and this was a decidedly Greek influence, since in the classical Greek city the control and performance of religious worship was open to every citizen, whereas in the east in general they were the prerogative of a priestly caste. Thus the cult of Serapis represents a genuine trend towards democratisation in which it is possible for all initiates to share in the benefits of close contact with the gods – a process that Christianity was to carry further. An even more significant departure from the older Egyptian religious ideas, prompted no doubt by the anxieties of the times, is the belief that a person's sharing of the gift of life is dependent on certain rites he performs during life, rather than on ceremonies carried out on his behalf after death. Man felt the need of protection and new life as much here as in the hereafter, and this is what the mystery religions were designed to offer. A prayer to the goddess Isis illustrates better than anything the personal and private nature of the relationship which the initiate felt and the support that this gave:

> Thou holy one, perpetual help of the human race, who are ever merciful to quicken the mortals, thou dost show to the poor in their misery the sweet tenderness of a mother. Not a day nor a night time rest, nor even a moment passes by without thy deeds of kindness, whereby thou dost watch over men on sea and land, driving away the storms of life and extending thy helping hand, with which thou dost untwist the inextricably tangled threads of destiny, dost calm the storms of fate and dost restrain the injurious courses of the stars . . . . Hence I will do what I can, one who is devout but in other respects poor. I will keep thy divine countenance and thy holy majesty for ever in the secret inner chambers of my breast and before my eyes.

Similar developments to the one we have just described for Egypt took place elsewhere also, it would seem. The Phrygian goddess Cybele, 'The Great Mother' and her consort Attis found their way to Rome as early as 205 B.C. at a time of particular crisis for the city, having been introduced to Athens almost two centuries earlier. This particular myth related how Cybele had fallen in love with the shepherd boy Attis, who, however, broke his vow to her and fell in love with a nymph, Sagaritis. Cybele killed the nymph but Attis went mad and in repentance castrated himself before being turned into a tree. However, he returned to life and toured triumphantly with the goddess. The pattern of death and resurrection is similar to the Isis/Osiris (Serapis) story and, on the understanding that myth and ritual are expressive of man's deepest concerns, we can detect in both stories the desire to overcome the anxieties of death, that the philosophical systems had dealt with but were not able to resolve satisfactorily. Part of the ritual of Attis involved orgiastic behaviour in which the initiates engaged in frenzied rites similar to those associated with the Greek god of wine, Dionysus. At first no Roman was allowed to take part in the worship since the priests were eunuchs and excesses of this kind did not commend themselves to the Roman temperament. In fact we know that the Dionysiac rites, which were very popular in the East, including Palestine, as we shall see, had been banned from Rome already in the second century B.C.E. – an indication of an early sensitivity there to oriental religions and something Christianity will also have to encounter. Nevertheless, during the reign of the Emperor Claudius (40-56 C.E.) at a time when Judaism was being banned from Rome by official edict (cf. Ac 18:2), the feast of Cybele became one of the great religious festivals at the capital continuing for six days, with public processions and other ceremonies. Clearly the mystery, once it had been prized free of its native setting was able to adapt and be assimilated into the lives of other people and places, while presumably still answering the religious needs of the times. It was this aspect of the mystery religions that ensured their popularity, just when acceptance of 'official' religion was on the decline.

Another Eastern mystery that was destined to travel west as far as Britain was the cult of the god Mithras. Its origins go back to Persian times, and with its notion of the seven spheres through which the soul must pass on its journey to union with god it had some contacts with Babylonian astrological speculation. The founding myth of Mithraism differed from those of Serapis and Cybele in that there is no question of the death and revivification of the hero. Instead Mithras is the great god of light who slew a white cosmic bull, thus releasing creative energy into the world. Mithras had a very distinctive moral character, exemplified by such symbols as fire, water, honey and the repeated emphasis of the sect on light and brightness. Despite the affirmation of the present creation in the myth the religion had developed an elaborate system of seven stages of perfection through which the soul of the individual had to pass in its struggle with evil (probably paralleling the god's initial struggle with the bull). Thus there was particular emphasis on moral attributes accompanied by an initiatory rite suited to each stage. A very definite hierarchy of authority operated within each unit or cell of the cult, which was not publicly organised but was based on moral attainment of the members within the group, the father of the cell being the one who had achieved the highest degree of perfection within the orders. Death, apparently, was not to be feared since it represented the final release of the soul and the attainment of its proper goal, yet on the other hand there is no frenzied rejection of the world as evil since it owed its origins to the creative action of Mithras.

It is not surprising therefore to find that when eventually Mithraism made its major impact on the Roman world (from the second to the fourth centuries C.E.), it had special appeal for the army and imperial bureaucratic officials whose task it was to ensure the continuance of the order that was Rome. The moral values so highly prized by the sect such as loyalty, obedience, commitment to legitimate authority and the like, were ideally suited to create loyal and trustworthy servants of the regime. It was also very popular in large aristocratic families, where its hierarchical structure corresponded to the already existing order and it encouraged the necessary virtues of loyalty, honesty and co-operation among the various levels of servants and slaves. It is therefore a classic case of a religion that had its origins in the East, but had been thoroughly adapted as it made its journey westward. As a result of this total identification with the Roman regime it seems to have had little impact on its own original oriental environment. It is tempting to make a comparison with the development of

Christianity which was eventually to become the official religion of the Empire. One is reminded of Paul's admonition to Roman Christians 'to obey the authorities that are over them, for there is no authority except from God' (Rm 13:1ff). The fact that Christians did not always follow this advice, or at least were thought by the authorities not to have done so, may be one reason why it, rather than Mithraism, was able to survive the fall of Rome. It did not pattern itself totally on a social order that was destined to pass away, and so emerged, scathed, but still intact from the dark ages.

This discussion of the mystery religions and their appeal as a phenomenon of the hellenistic and Roman religious world, is not intended to suggest that Christianity is a similar development, or that it is simply an outgrowth of these cults. There are many interesting parallels, and yet there are just as many striking differences. More important than the details, however, is the fact that in all these various movements – Christianity included – certain basic patterns of man's religious experience can be readily discerned. These can be enumerated as follows: 1) A myth or story of the gods' dealing with man and the world, which answers some fundamental question about life and offers the possibility of overcoming a particular feeling of alienation or dislocation at the level of everyday experience. 2) An initiatory rite in which, usually after a process of preparation, the individual was allowed into close communion with the god, sharing in the redemptive power of the myth and receiving special knowledge of the heavenly realm. 3) A ritual re-enactment of the myth, whereby periodically the group of initiates relived their initiatory experience and shared anew its saving power. It should also be noted that the mysteries were capable of adapting to the changing needs of the times and of their devotees. There was no rivalry between them and apparently no network of communication between the units of the same cult in different cities. Indeed in later times, and possibly due to the influence of Christian and Jewish monotheism, the tendency was to identify the gods of the various cults or treat them as manifestations of the universal religion of all men. In these regards both Christianity and Judaism were very different. One has only to think of the constant greetings from members of different house churches to those in other cities at the end of all of Paul's letters and the constancy with which Jewish believers throughout the world supported their cult centre at Jerusalem. Nevertheless, when Paul describes Baptism, the Christian's rite of initiation, as a dying and rising with Christ (Rm 6:2-4), that is, embodying the saving-event for the new believer, it is not difficult to see that the pattern is the same as that of the mysteries. Similarly, the celebration of the Eucharist, 'as a proclaiming of the Lord's death until he comes' (1 Cor 11:26), can be seen as the re-presentation of the saving death of Jesus. The fact that later the Eucharist was called the 'Arcanum' or 'hidden mystery' by Christians, presumably because of its secret celebration, could only add to the impression at least for outsiders, that Christianity was just another mystery religion.

Conclusion

Our review of the Greek influence that continued to shape the social and religious world of the New Testament, has necessarily been sketchy. However, it should be clear that the early Christian religious experience, and its literary expression in the New Testament clearly reflects many of the aspects we have been discussing. Christians were indeed real people in a real world which was characterised by social change, mobility of population and religious and philosophical questioning, occasioned by the political and other upheavals taking place. Much of this influence was to work to the advantage of Christianity, from the common language and the possibility of wholesale travel to the elaboration of philosophical systems and moral values that had genuine affinities with the Christian world-view. Yet as late as the third century of the Christian era there was still quite a body of opinion abroad that claimed it was possible through rational contemplation alone to understand the universe and its relation to the one God. This legacy was only finally appropriated by the Christian schoolmen of the middle ages who were able to achieve the proper blend of Greek rationalism and Christian revelation, thereby ensuring its lasting place within the history of human civilisation and enormously enriching the intellectual dimension of Christian faith. But that was long after the period currently under review. In stressing the many formative influences of the hellenistic legacy on early Christianity, we are not of course questioning the uniqueness of the Christian response to its world. However, hopefully these influences serve to underline the incarnational aspect of Christian faith as exemplified in its founder Jesus of Nazareth, the Word made flesh. It should be no surprise that the same pattern is continued as the church carried its good news from Jerusalem to Rome, and beyond.

2. The Roman World

2. THE ROMAN WORLD

Judas had heard of the reputation of the Romans. They were valiant fighters and acted amiably to all who took their side . . . He was also told of their battles and the brave deeds that they had performed against the Gauls, conquering them and forcing them to pay tribute . . . Philip and Perseus, king of the Macedonians . . . had been overwhelmed and subjugated . . . Antiochus, the Great king of Asia . . . had been defeated by them. They had taken him alive and obliged him and the kings who succeeded him to pay a heavy tribute . . . When the men of Greece had planned to come and destroy them, the Romans discovered it and sent against the Greeks a single general who made war on them. Many were wounded and fell, and the Romans took their wives and children captive . . . Yet with all this none of them put on a crown or wore purple as a display of grandeur. They had made for themselves a senate house, and every day three hundred and twenty men took counsel, deliberating on all that concerned the people and their well being. So Judas chose Eupolemus . . . and Jason . . . and sent them to Rome to establish an alliance of friendship with them (1 Macc 8:1-17).

In those days Caesar Augustus published a decree that the whole world should be enrolled. This first census took place while Quirinius was governor of Syria (Lk 2:1).

In the fifteenth year of the rule of Tiberius Caesar, when Pontius Pilate was procurator of Judea, Herod tetrarch of Galilee, Philip his brother, tetrarch of the region of Ituraea and Trachonitis, and Lysanias tetrarch of Abilene, during the high priesthood of Annas and Caiaphas, the word of God was spoken to John son of Zechariah in the desert (Lk 3:1-2).

Render to Caesar what is Caesar's and to God what is God's (Mk 12:17).

If we let him go on like this, the whole world will believe in him. Then the Romans will come in and sweep away our sanctuary and our nation (Jn 11:48).

If you free this man you are no 'friend of Caesar'. Anyone who makes himself a king becomes Caesar's rival (Jn 19:12).

I (Paul) stand before the imperial bench. That is where I must be tried . . . Therefore Festus conferred with his council and finally declared: "You have appealed to the Emperor. To the Emperor you shall go" (Ac 25:10-12).

I am under obligation to Greeks and non-Greeks, to learned and unintelligent alike. That is why I am eager to preach the gospel to you Romans as well (Rm 1:14f).

Now I have no more work to do in these regions, and I continue to cherish the desire to visit you which I have had for many years. As soon as I can set out for Spain I hope to see you in passing (Rm 15:23-24).

On her forehead was written a symbolic name, "Babylon the great, mother of harlots and all the world's abominations". I saw that the woman was drunk with the blood of God's holy ones and the blood of those martyred for their faith in Jesus (Rev 17:5-6).

IN THE PREVIOUS chapter we have noted more than once that the Greek heritage – cultural, legal and religious – was encountered by the early Christians in and through the institutions of the Roman Empire. This is not to suggest that the Romans were merely borrowers in these and other fields of human endeavour; it does mean that for the first Christians the most immediate and concrete reality of life was Roman government and administration. In other words, the outward form of early Christianity's world was undeniably Roman, even if the heart and soul was Greek, or alternatively Jewish, as we shall see in the next chapter. It is on this external world of Emperors and Governors, legal prosecutions and personal and community rights that we wish to focus in this chapter, since it is within these structures that early Christianity emerged and developed. The chain of citations which we have given at the outset (including the *First Book of Maccabees*) suggests that the relationship could vary considerably. From being the ally and friend of the weak in the first citation Rome becomes the whore of Babylon, the murderer of the faithful, in the final one. We shall examine the various phases of the relationship by considering the way in which Rome came to control the Mediterranean (I), the manner in which its imperial designs were likely to run counter to Jewish national aspirations in Palestine (II) and the legal status of Jews (and Christians) in the Diaspora (III).

I. The Roman Political Scene During the First Century of the Common Era.

In striking contrast to the startling rapidity of Alexander's campaigns by which in the space of ten short years he conquered the Middle East from the Mediterranean to the Indus, the advance of Rome was slow, piecemeal and sometimes even fortuitous. So impressed was the Greek historian Polybius with the gradual but inevitable process of the development, already in the second century B.C.E., that he declared that Fate had determined that Rome should rule the world. The steady expansion of the Roman *imperium* or rule over two centuries was ultimately to stand the test of time better than Alexander's striking successes. Certainly, by the first century their achievement must have appeared both inevitable and eternal for the Romans themselves. One of their great poets, Horace, speaking of his own works, writes: 'I have raised up a monument more lasting than bronze. As long as high priest with silent step ascends the Capitol my songs will be sung'. Even second century Christian apologists saw the peace that came to the world with the rise of Augustus, the *pax Augusta* as it was called, as providentially arranged by God in preparation for Christianity. Earlier, another Roman poet, Virgil, in his famous fourth Eclogue had spoken of the times in language and imagery strangely similar to Jewish messianic hopes, especially the famous Emmanuel prophecy of Isaiah that had been appropriated by the Christians for their own leader, Jesus:

> Under thy guidance whatso tracks remain of our old wickedness, once done away, shall free the earth from never-ceasing fear. He shall receive the life of gods, and see heroes with gods commingling, and himself be seen of them, and with his father's worth reign o'er a world at peace.

While the reign of Augustus was not entirely free of wars, especially on the northern frontiers where the Germanic tribes were a constant threat, it certainly came nearest to the realisation of these dreams. Towards the end of his career Augustus was able to boast that three times during his reign the senate had decreed that the temple of Janus, the god of the door, be shut. This symbolic action had only been performed twice before in Roman history – after the first Punic War and after the battle of Actium in 31 B.C.E.

Rome is the only example in history of a single city-state growing to a world empire. This extraordinary feat can be attributed to a combination of military skill and courage, a pragmatic philosophy that was prepared to extend its citizenship indefinitely as a reward for loyalty and service, and by a political shrewdness that was able to improvise executive and administrative arrangements to meet the particular needs of any situation. The first stages of her advancement within the Italian peninsula were slow and hazardous, beginning with a defense of her own territories and then adopting the role of aggressor as she pushed southwards in the peninsula, but already the pattern for future success was established by the way in which the cities and territories that had been conquered were incorporated into the expanding net – now by treaty of alliance, now by colonisation and again by the grant of citizenship. It was in this push to the south that Rome came into contact with Carthage, a naval outpost of the Phoenicians in North Africa, just across from Sicily, and the two rival commercial and military powers became embroiled in a lengthy confrontation, known as the two Punic Wars (264-241 B.C.E. and 218-202 B.C.E.) that ended with the defeat of the famous general Hannibal, the destruction of Carthage and the establishment of Rome as the dominant force in the western Mediterranean.

The Punic wars were an important milestone in Roman military history. New techniques and weapons of war were developed and above all a competent naval force that was fit and eager to take on the best that the hellenistic monarchies of the east had to offer. Perhaps the most important effect of all for the future was the emergence of the provincial system whereby conquered territory was organised under Roman rule. At the end of the first Punic War, Sicily was so constituted with its own governor sent annually by Rome. The excerpt from the first book of Maccabees, cited at the beginning of this chapter, is really a catalogue of her successes throughout the second century B.C.E. as Rome extended her influence eastward. Macedonia, Asia (part of modern Turkey), North Africa were all conquered and organised as provinces by the year 133 B.C.E. It was only in the next century that Syria (in 63) and Egypt (in 31) were finally added to the list of Roman provinces in the East, making the Euphrates river the eastern boundary of the Empire. Consequently the Roman conquest never went as far as that of Alexander. This had repercussions for Palestine, since it was to be one of several important buffer states along the borders with Rome's great rival in the East, the Parthians, and Rome had to ensure that at all times this small but strategically important land was firmly in its control.

Naturally, the character of Roman life had changed considerably in the two centuries of conquest and expansion. Unlike the east, where the tradition of monarchy had a long and noble history, Rome had already abolished the kingship in 510 B.C.E., opting instead for an aristocratic republic. Even when eventually in the first century B.C.E. the Emperor became absolute monarch in all but name, he was technically known as 'princeps', that is first among equals, and in theory at least he held his position at the behest of the Roman senate. Originally the senate, consisting of members of the patrician or aristocratic families, selected two officers annually, the consuls, to run the affairs of state; but at a relatively early date, the plebeians or second order, had obtained some measure of involvement, even to the point of being eligible for the office of consul. We have already met the equestrian order of knights in the previous chapter, who technically were plebeians rather than patricians, but who through the new wealth and the gradual demise of the old aristocracy due to civil strife and various purges, became very influential in the later Republican and Imperial times. There was however great social unrest in Roman society among the lower classes, especially slaves, freedmen and provincials. Various attempts at reform had been ineffectual, or were blocked, notably that of the Gracchi which sought a fairer distribution of the public land and the stabilisation of prices in Rome. Another reform achieved only after a bitter war was the granting of full citizenship to all the Italians. By the first century a full-scale civil war situation prevailed between the old aristocracy and the rising middle class. The power now gradually shifted to the military men who were warding off the enemies of Rome at the frontiers and at the same time vieing for power and influence at the centre. The armies were now no longer recruited from the peasant farming stock but instead soldiering had become a professional art, and the foreign wars – in the east against Mithridates and in the west in Spain and Gaul – gave the species of legitimacy to the several armed forces that were maintained. The final years of the Republic were marked by this bitter in-fighting – the period of the Triumvirates – which inevitably ended in a struggle for power between two of the three who had entered into an alliance. First it was the struggle between Pompey (the conqueror of Palestine, as we shall see) and Caesar, with the latter emerging as sole dictator after the battle of Pharsalus in 48 B.C.E. However his murder in 44 B.C.E. by Brutus and Cassius, who were the remnants of the old aristocratic class that had been swept aside in the struggle for power, gave rise to the second triumvirate and the inevitable struggle between Mark Antony (Cleopatra's lover) and Octavian (Caesar's adopted son, the future Augustus). The matter was finally resolved in 31 B.C.E. with Octavian successful at the battle of Actium, a victory that marked the end of the Roman Republic and the formal beginning of the Principate, as it was originally called.

However, Octavian, or Augustus, as he came to be known when a decree of the Roman government conferred this name with its honorific overtones on him in 27 B.C.E., moved cautiously, realising the fate of his foster father, Caesar. The Senate also conferred on him control of certain provinces – Spain, Gaul, Syria and Egypt – those where the largest portion of the army was located, and this ensured his power base. It was further formally decreed that he could declare war, conclude treaties and do 'whatever he may deem to serve the interest of the Republic'. He was named *'Pontifex Maximus'*. 'High Priest', in 12 B.C.E. and *'Pater Patriae'*, 'father of the fatherland' in 2 B.C.E. However, not all the subsequent Emperors (the title *Imperator* was originally a military one: 'head of the armed forces') treated the senate with the same respect. Tiberius, Augustus' successor, withdrew to the island of Capri and conducted the affairs of state from that retreat, surrounded by his own favourites and advisers, and the senate had either lost the will or the interest to complain about such derogation of its powers. This was particularly true of the Emperors Gaius (Caligula) (37-41) and Nero (51-64), both of whose careers were to be of special interest to Jews and Christians, as we shall see.

In controlling this vast territory that comprised the Empire we catch a glimpse of Roman administrative skills. The provincial system had been developed already under the Republic, but now a distinction was made between Senatorial and Imperial provinces as new territories were organised: Egypt (30 B.C.E.); Galatia (25 B.C.E.); Raetia and Noricum (15 B.C.E.); Judaea (6 C.E.); Cappadocia (17 C.E.); Britain (43 C.E.); Arabia (107 C.E.). The former, like Sicily and Africa, were under the direct control of the senate, who appointed the governors, whereas the latter, for example Syria, were the places where the military legions were deployed for security or other reasons and under the direct control of the Emperor. Depending on the status of the province the governor came from senatorial or equestrian rank – this latter being the case in Judaea. Apparently the governors of senatorial rank had some rights of supervision over those of equestrian background, since there are several instances of the governor of Syria directly intervening in Palestinian affairs, and this is reflected in the New Testament also where the census of Quirinius, governor of Syria is mentioned and Pontius

Pilate is called *Procurator* of Judaea, a title that indicates lower rank to governor.

In theory at least the provincial system was intended to allow for local customs and culture to have their say, and this was part of the Roman genius. However, in reality very often there was too much opportunity for corruption and venality. The term of office was too short and the temptation to capitalise on the provincials was very great for somebody intending to return to the capital shortly. In effect he was an autocrat, and his decisions, even in matters of capital punishment, were final except in extraordinary circumstances, a fact that has particular relevance for understanding the trials of Jesus and Paul in the New Testament. Judaea certainly had its share of such procurators, drawn, as we have mentioned, from the middle class equestrians. Indeed the mismanagement of Judaean affairs by the procurators especially after 44 C.E. was one of the chief contributory factors to the first Jewish revolt of 66-70. In all, three of these equestrian procurators of Judaea are mentioned in the New Testament – Pontius Pilate (gospels), Porcius Festus and Felix (*Acts of the Apostles*) – and as we shall see, all three fit well the profile one could anticipate from their background. One of them, Felix, was the brother of Pallas, a close associate and advisor of the Emperor Claudius, so one can imagine the sense of freedom with which he approached the task of governing 'the unruly' Jews. Apart from Quirinius, the governor of Syria of senatorial rank mentioned in connection with the census, we also meet two governors of senatorial provinces in *Acts*: Sergius Paulus in Cyprus and Annius Gallio at Corinth. An inscription found at Delphi bearing the name of this latter makes it possible to date his office with a high degree of probability to the year 51 C.E., and so this gives us some important external confirmation for dating Paul's career.

Apart from the provincial system another facet of Roman administration that is important for New Testament times is the system of 'client kings'. As already mentioned, kingship had a long tradition in the East, and it is altogether in keeping with Roman policies to allow these to continue – provided they did not interfere with her own dynastic intentions. An excellent example of the way in which this system worked is the family of the Herods in Judaea. The family originally came to prominence under Caesar when Antipater, a half-Jew from Idumaea (southern Palestine), was entrusted with the control of the financial affairs in the recently carved-up territory of the Jews. However, it was his younger son Herod who received the title 'king, friend and ally of the Roman people', by a decree of the senate in 40 B.C.E. as reward for his support of Mark Antony in the civil war after Caesar's death. An additional incentive from the Roman point of view was the fact that their great rivals in the East, the Parthians, had invaded Palestine and supported one of the deposed Hasmonaeans, Antigonus, as king. Herod eventually conquered his recently acquired kingdom and was in complete control of the internal affairs of Judaea until his death in 4 B.C.E., paying an annual tribute to the Roman coffers for the honour of kingship. On Herod's death, and despite his last will, his territory was carved up among three surviving sons –Archelaus, Antipas and Philip, but none of them ever received the title king, despite the fact that Mark calls Antipas 'king' on the occasion of the birthday celebration when John the Baptist was beheaded (Mk 6:14). Both Matthew and Luke are familiar with his official title, 'tetrarch', literally 'ruler of a quarter' (Mt 14:1; Lk 9:7), however, Herod's grandson, Herod Agrippa I, who had been brought up in Imperial court circles and was a close friend of the Emperor Gaius (Caligula) received the title king and ruled over part of Palestine from 37 C.E., and the whole from 41 C.E. until his death in 44 C.E., when the territory reverted to the provincial status once more. While Agrippa was beloved by the Jews as a devout and good king, mediating with the Romans on a number of important issues, he treated Palestinian Christians badly, having James the apostle put to death. His own sudden death is seen by the author of Acts (12:1-20) as a just punishment by God. Subsequently, his son Agrippa II, though never enjoying the same territorial control as his father, was also recognised as king, and like his father, attempted to play the intermediary between Rome and the Jews at the time of the first revolt (cf. Ac 25:13-26:32). The Herods were not the only client kings whom Rome supported in the East since we hear of a similar arrangement in Armenia, Cappadocia and Comagene. However they were quick to recognise any signs of insubordination and return to the provincial system by which the Emperor bestowed the right to rule directly on a Roman, who then enjoyed full power to direct the affairs of the province as he wished, always subject to the superior authority of the Emperor, of course.

This raises the question already mentioned in connection with the trials of Jesus and Paul, namely, the rights of Roman citizens as distinct from those of *peregrini*, as the provincials were called. In terms of the New Testament, how was it that Paul was able to have his case transferred from the provincial tribunal of Festus to Rome whereas no such option was apparently open to Jesus? In invoking what is technically called *provocatio*, which should not be confused with an appeal from a lower to higher court, Paul clearly relies on his Roman citizenship (Ac 16:37; 25:10-12). This gave him special privileges in regard to criminal processes, at least at an earlier period, before citizenship was extended on a fairly large scale to the provincials and the wholesale transfer of cases to the capital was no longer feasible. At Philippi, for example, a Roman colony, Paul having been accused of subverting the Roman citizens of the town, was thrown into prison after having been flogged. Paul was indignant at this treatment of Roman citizens and the magistrates were quite upset on finding out his status (Ac 16:19-40). Again, Claudius Lysias, the commander who was cross-examining Paul after his arrest in Jerusalem was surprised to find out that he was a Roman citizen, and his whole approach to Paul changed considerably once he recognised that they were both on equal footing. Paul had been born with citizen's rights, whereas Claudius had had to purchase his, probably through bribery of some Roman bureaucrats (Ac 22:22-29). Subsequently the governor Festus, and Agrippa II, whom the governor consulted on the matter, upheld Paul's claims and treated him with great caution, even respect (Ac 25:12-25; 26:32). When one contrasts this treatment with that of Jesus by Pontius Pilate, being a Roman citizen was clearly a distinct advantage in the first century C.E., at least in cases where no clearcut crime had been committed in terms of the Roman *ordo*.

Citizenship was not automatically conferred on the subjects of conquered territories. The inhabitants of the Italian peninsula only received it after a bitter struggle. Various conquering generals were given the right to confer citizenship on those whom they considered fit, and of course the Emperor could also do the same. Usually, the new citizen took the name of his patron – the Claudius Lysias of Acts, for example, had obviously received his from the Emperor Claudius. Paul on the other hand says that he was born a Roman citizen – which means that his father, or some earlier generation still had received it, but we have no indication of the circumstances or from whom it was received, and the name Paul does not give us any clue, since it is a rare name among Roman patrician families. Apparently, citizenship in the eastern provinces was not granted as readily as in the West, where it was an extension of the rights granted to the Italians at a relatively early date. Consequently, Roman citizens formed a small but important enclave in the East in Paul's day, especially outside the few colonies that Rome had directly founded: Corinth, Philippi, Troas in Greece and Antioch in Pisidia and Lystra in Asia, all on important trade routes, and so visited by Paul on his journeys. One gets the impression that the Roman magistrates are rather surprised to find out Paul's citizenship, since in their experience such a man might be expected to be a ranking officer in the Roman army or magistrate in his native city, especially Tarsus, which had quite a reputation as an intellectual centre.

In sketching this outline of the Roman political and administrative scene in the first century C.E. we have concentrated on those aspects that directly affected both Jews and Christians. For the Romans there was scarcely any distinction, at least in the earlier period, when early christianity was likely to have been dealt with within the structures created by Rome to deal with Jewish faith and practice. Consequently, we must now examine in greater detail Rome's dealings with Jews, first in Palestine and then in the wider Diaspora, if we are to understand the full impact Rome had in shaping the world of the early Christians.

II. Rome and the Jews in Palestine

The passage from 1 Macc quoted at the beginning of this chapter shows how the Jews first envisaged Rome's presence in the East. She was their ally, supporting Jewish efforts to cast off the yoke of the hellenistic monarchies – at that time the Seleucids of Syria, who had attempted to wipe out the Jewish religion altogether by the infamous decree of 167 B.C.E., to be examined in our next chapter. Through a combination of daring military exploits and internal troubles of the Seleucid house, the Jews, under the Maccabaean brothers and their successors were able to establish an independent state, the Hasmonaean state as it is called, that included within its boundaries all of Palestine west of the Jordan with the exception of the Phoenician coastal cities, as well as a good deal of Transjordan, both north and south. The fact that the Seleucids were forced to pay a large war indemnity annually to the Romans ever since the battle of Magnesium in 190 B.C.E. was one contributory factor to the weakness of the Seleucids, though it also explains their continued attempts to squeeze the last shekel from the Jewish territory, even at one point violating the sanctuary in Jerusalem in order to rob it of its sacred vessels. Rome was not averse to a strong Jewish state, since it could act as a check on either Seleucid or Ptolemaic ambitions, never totally abandoned, to restore the Empire of Alexander. Thus it was that for the last time until our own century the Jews were able to establish their own state for a period of approximately 70 years, from 142 B.C.E., when final tax concessions were won from the Seleucids, to 63 B.C.E. when the Romans intervened directly in Palestinian affairs.

In 63 B.C.E. Pompey, who was just then engaged in settling the affairs of the East and clearing the Mediterranean of pirates, acceded to the request of a Jewish delegation who wanted him to resolve a dispute between two Hasmonaean brothers as to which of them should be king. It was quite a natural request given the longstanding friendship between the two peoples. However, Pompey availed of the opportunity to carve up the Hasmonaean kingdom, restoring their freedom to a number of hellenistic cities and leaving three separated territories – Judaea (around Jerusalem), Galilee (in the north) and Peraea (across the Jordan) in the hands of the Jews, ruled over by the high priest Hyrcanus II (one of the rival claimants) an ethnarch, not king, and with Antipater as his financial controller. Pompey actually invaded the temple in Jerusalem and entered the Holy of Holies, to the great horror of pious Jews, but unlike the Seleucid King, Antiochus IV, who also violated the sanctuary almost a hundred years earlier, he did not rob the temple of its precious objects. Yet his action suggested that a new era in Jewish-Roman relations had begun in which Jewish hopes and aspirations would have to take second place to the designs of Roman imperialism. This was confirmed a few years later by

Gabinius, the governor of Syria, who pressed ahead with an even more thorough division of the country. Caesar improved the situation somewhat by granting the Jews some tax concessions in deference to their religious obligations of the sabbatical year, and he restored Hyrcanus as head of all the Jewish territory and declared him entitled to receive the tithes. Yet his settlement, confirmed by Mark Antony after his death, made the Jews the unequal partner. Rome was from now on to remain directly in charge of Jewish fortunes, and her authority would always be supreme.

We have already mentioned the rise of Herod, Antipater's son, who succeeded in playing his political cards cleverly throughout the difficult years of the triumvirates and was rewarded by Rome with the kingship of Judaea. This was a bitter pill for the Jews to swallow – an Idumaean, half-Jew in complete control of their affairs, both saecular and religious. Once established, Herod was not slow to assert himself: the older priestly aristocracy was purged, the high priest, Hyrcanus II, was deposed and replaced by candidates of Herod's own choosing, and the Sanhedrin was denuded of all its powers as the supreme governing body of the nation. Herod was no mindless monster however, despite his avowed hellenistic policies abroad. As part of his building projects, the temple in Jerusalem was to be rebuilt, something that came quickly to the mind of Jesus' audience a generation later when it appeared as though he were threatening the temple (Jn 2:18-22). Not only was it the central symbol of their belief, it was also the source of economic stability for many Jerusalemites and Herod's reconstruction policy served the dual purpose of placating his Jewish subjects' religious loyalties and generating extra jobs within his realm. People were less antagonised by the heavy burden of taxes and the spending abroad when there were some visible signs of how their contributions were being used, and besides the large work-force gainfully employed was likely to be more submissive. Despite his shrewdness however, the last years of Herod's reign were marked by a growing paranoia about his successor, and even his own family was not spared the threat of execution as plots, real or imagined, were 'discovered', and those suspected eliminated. Though there is no evidence in our other sources about the slaughter of the Innocents reported by Matthew (2:16-18), and historians have questioned its likelihood, at least on the scale reported, there is no doubt but that the Evangelist shows Herod's character correctly. He may have wished to ironically suggest to his readers, and no doubt the point was not lost on those who were Jews, that Jesus posed a far greater threat to Herod's kingship than any of those who sought his crown.

So oppressive was Herod's rule that on his death fifty leading men of the Jews appeared before Augustus and asked to have the Herodian dynasty set aside and Judaea incorporated into the province of Syria. While they and the surviving claimants were debating their case in Rome, serious trouble had broken out in Palestine – the first in a series of violent episodes that were to dominate Palestinian life for the next century. Apparently, resistance had been driven underground rather than eradicated during the long reign of Herod, and now at the first opportunity these elements erupted in a spontaneous display of independence at the feasts of Passover and Pentecost. National loyalties were fanned by the flames of religious fervour, and first Archelaus (before his departure for Rome), and subsequently the Roman legate of Syria, Varus, put down the revolt with great brutality, underlining what Matthew tells us about Archelaus being as brutal as his father Herod (Mt 2:22). As already touched on, Herod's kingdom was now divided between Archelaus (Judaea), Antipas (Galilee and Peraea) and Philip (Trachonitis and Batanaea), the first step in the provincialisation of Palestine by the Romans (cf. Lk 3:1). Ten years later (4 B.C.E. – 6 C.E.) Archelaus, because of continued unrest in his territory, was deposed and Judaea made into an imperial province of equestrian rank, with the procurator living at Caesarea on the coast – a city founded by Herod and thoroughly Graeco-Roman in its style and atmosphere (cf. Ac 24:1; 25:1.13), something that recent archaeology of the site has confirmed.

Except for the short period of Herod Agrippa I's reign (37-44 C.E.), Judaea was to remain a Roman province (enlarged by the addition of Galilee in 44 C.E.). Thus direct Roman rule and the animosity it generated among the Jews was experienced in the south to a greater extent than in Galilee, a fact that explains the frequency of the Zealots' presence in the former province during the next half century or more. This consideration is important as it is frequently asserted that Galilee was the hot-bed of Jewish nationalism in the first century, even to the point of making Jesus and his followers into an armed band of revolutionaries. The fact that Judas the Galilean, mentioned in Ac 5:37 as having unsuccessfully attempted a revolution against Rome in 6 C.E., is presumed to have come from the province, lends a specious legitimacy to these assumptions. In fact it was in Jerusalem that Judas launched his call to freedom and the refusal to pay tribute to any human master, as the Romans initiated a census of the newly formed province for direct taxation purposes. It remains unproven that his revolutionary ideas were originally fostered in his home-land, where there was no similar disturbance when it was incorporated into the Roman provincial system in 44 C.E. In fact Herod Antipas, the Herod of John's beheading (Mk 6:15-30) and Jesus' trial (Lk 23:7-12), appears to have given some degree of stability to Galilean life. Though Jesus seems to have avoided the cities of his residences, Sepphoris, four miles north-east of Nazareth, and Tiberias, which he founded on the lake front, the reason may not have been just fear of arrest (Lk 13:31). It was not without cause that Antipas had earned the name 'fox' (Lk 13:32), probably referring to his astuteness in obtaining the position of ruler without meriting it, in contrast to the lion who was really the king of the animals. Antipas was not likely to engage in any activity that would disturb the peace and draw down the wrath of the Romans after their treatment of Archelaus, and Jesus was undoubtedly popular with the Galilean crowds, at least initially. According to Josephus the beheading of John the Baptist, a Judaean not a Galilean figure in the gospels, took place because John was a political threat, and was not just the result of a drunken whim, as the gospels suggest. Furthermore, the episode is located by Josephus in Machaerus, a fortress in Peraea, and not in Galilee, where the population was probably more mixed and resistance less likely from a largely rural and peasant people.

The New Testament mentions three of the Roman procurators of Judaea in the period between 6 and 66 C.E. – Pilate from 26-36 C.E., Felix 52-60 C.E. and Festus 60-62 C.E. The normal period of office appears to have been two years, but obviously there was considerable flexibility depending on various circumstances, such as the policy of the Emperor, influential friends at Rome and one's performance in the province. It was important for a procurator to establish good relations with some at least of the more influential elements in his province and it is not surprising to find Herod Agrippa II and his wife Berenice paying an official visit to the newly arrived Festus, and the latter defers suitably by having Agrippa also hear Paul's case (Ac 25:13-26:32). Felix had actually married Drusilla, the daughter of Agrippa I, a Jewess (Ac 24:24) who had abandoned her previous husband for him.

The procurators of Judaea were in charge of the military personnel in the province. In the case of Judaea, there were no Roman legions stationed there, though they were ready at hand for any disturbances and were often called upon. After the great revolt had been put down in 70 C.E. one legion, the *decima X Fretensis*, was stationed in the great plain at the ancient strategic site of Megiddo. Whereas the legions were made up entirely of Roman citizens, this was not necessarily true of the auxiliaries that were permanently stationed in Palestine. These were apparently often recruited from the non-Jewish population of Palestine and

Syria, and as can be expected, were for the most part resented, and they in turn showed their contempt for things Jewish, to the point where a Roman soldier actually profaned the Temple during a festival with an indecent act. The treatment of Jesus by the soldiers during the trial is perfectly true to life, even when the Evangelists see it as fulfilment of Old Testament Scriptures dealing with the suffering of the just man (e.g. Mt 27:30.35.43; Jn 19:24.36). However, we do meet some exceptions. Cornelius, the centurion who eventually became a Christian, was a 'sympathiser', and so apparently were other soldiers of his unit (Ac 10:7). This means that they had probably some association, possibly as 'God-fearers,' as such gentiles were called, with the Jewish synagogue. It may be no coincidence that he was from the Italian cohort (Ac 10:1), that is that he was not a native Palestinian, and so not heir to the prejudices and mutual recriminations that had been building up for a century or more in that region.

One general question about the procurators that has been much discussed is their role in judicial matters. We have already confirmed that Paul was perfectly within his rights as a Roman citizen in asking to have his case transferred to Rome, but this does not mean that the procurators did not have the right to impose capital punishment within their province without any right of appeal. This is clear from the trial and crucifixion of Jesus, crucifixion being the Roman form of inflicting the death penalty, which shows that they took full legal responsibility for it in his case. There are plenty of other instances from this period where offenders who could be regarded as 'political' were executed within the province also: Theudas, a Jewish rebel who is put on a par with Judas the Galilean (Ac 5:37) and was put to death by Cuspius Fadus the procurator from 44-46 C.E., while his successor Tiberius Alexander, himself an Egyptian Jew in the Imperial service, executed the two sons of Judas the Galilean, presumably for espousing their father's philosophy of rejection of Roman rule. Apparently the procurator could also waive his right to try a particular

case and send it to Rome, and there are examples of this
procedure also, but from the cases in question there does
not appear to have been a definite policy on the matter.
A complicating factor in the case of Judaea is the compe-
tency of the Jewish Sanhedrin to pass the death sentence.
Unfortunately, this very intriguing question of ancient
legal history has become embroiled in later polemics, in
which the Jews have been accused by Christians of killing
their Messiah, and Jewish scholarship has, understandably,
reacted by denying that the Jewish people had any such
authority at that time – something the Gospel of John would
seem to put beyond doubt by the answer of the Jewish
leaders to Pilate: 'We may not put anyone to death' (Jn
18:31).

The tractate Sanhedrin in the Mishnah, the Jewish law
code, does recognise that it has the power of life and death,
but, it is claimed, this reflects a much later idealised view
of the Sanhedrin and does not reflect the first century
situation. As against this statement in John it has been
pointed out that the Sanhedrin passed sentence of death on
Stephen (Ac 6:15), and Josephus tells us that during the
interregnum between the procuratorships of Festus and
Albinus, that is in 62 C.E., James, the brother of the Lord
and head of the Jerusalem Christian Church, together
with some others, was condemned to death by stoning by the
Sanhedrin. However, it should be noted that Stephen's
death has more the appearance of mob lynching than a
formal execution (Ac 7:54-60), and the high priest who had
James put to death was reported to the incoming procurator
by moderate Jews and subsequently deposed for his action.
On the other hand several inscriptions found in the temple
area of Jerusalem threaten death to any gentile who
passed beyond a certain point and it should be noted that
Stephen was accused of 'speaking against the holy place'
(Ac 6:13). Paul, also, was on trial for his life when the
Romans intervened, and one of the charges was that the
Jews suspected him of bringing a gentile, Trophimus of

Ephesus, into the temple precincts (Ac 21:29). In fact Festus wanted him to be tried by the Sanhedrin, but Paul refused and at that point decided to make his appeal to Rome (Ac 25:9-12). It seems reasonable to suppose therefore that the Sanhedrin did have certain well-circumscribed rights to impose the capital sentence when the temple was expressly under attack, and different Roman procurators may have exercised varying degrees of vigilance over the way in which this right was exercised.

This brings us back to the legalities of the trial of Jesus. The gospel portrait of Pilate has sometimes been regarded as suspect, mainly because Josephus, our only other major source, presents him as a greedy and ruthless individual with little regard for the Jewish religion or practice. He is reported as having introduced images of Caesar into Jerusalem, always a sensitive issue with the Jews, because of the fear of idolatry and the second commandment prohibiting images of any kind. Besides, he appropriated money from the temple treasury to build an aqueduct into Jerusalem. On another occasion he broke up a religious gathering of the Samaritans with wholesale slaughter. Could this be the Pilate of the gospels, it is argued, who is presented as weak, even ineffectual perhaps, but not abrasive and arrogant? Those who think that it could not, believe that the gospels' portrait has been deliberately softened by early Christian tradition, anxious to curry favour with Rome by exonerating her from all blame for Jesus' death, whereas it is maintained, the crucifixion shows that it was Rome, not the Jews who were really responsible. However, to this it can be countered that in passing final judgement, Pilate would naturally impose the Roman form of sentence – crucifixion. Death by stoning would have been inconceivable in a Roman court, yet Pilate's involvement and decision was inevitable once the charge was made one of subversion of Roman law and order, something that Luke in particular underlines (Lk 23:2). In this instance Pilate was able to placate certain elements of the Jewish aristocracy, and according to Luke, also ingratiate himself with Antipas, by having the latter try Jesus as well (Lk 23:7-12), without compromising his own position in any way. Yet, it should be noted that Luke is aware of Pilate's true nature by referring in passing to an incident, otherwise unknown, concerning the slaughter of Galileans in Jerusalem (Lk 13:2). Given the differing purposes of their writings then, there is no real contradiction between Josephus' portrait of Pilate and the gospels' accounts, nor any improbability about the main lines of the latters' version of the charge against Jesus. The Jews referred the case to Pilate, even though it was within their general competence insofar as the charge allegedly involved an attack on the temple, because they were conscious of Pilate's likely reactions had they proceeded independently. At the same time they had to put the case in political, not religious terms, because of his indifference, even hostility to their religious feelings.

The other procurators mentioned in the New Testament, Felix and Festus, get off rather lightly in *Acts of the Apostles*, considering their records. At the end of Felix's term of office Judaea was in anarchy, as the Jewish resistance movement that had been partly underground for sometime now emerged in full light of day. The Judaean countryside seems to have been their base, though Jerusalem and the temple was their goal. In fact their name, *sicarii*, is probably derived from their tactic of using the small Roman *sica* or dagger disguised under their cloaks, as they engaged in what can be described as urban guerilla warfare. Not merely were they determined to overthrow the Romans for religious reasons, first stated emphatically by Judas the Galilean, but they also directed their ire against the wealthy Jewish aristocracy who were seen as collaborationists with Rome. Felix did nothing to control the situation, and may even have used the *sicarii* to murder a former high priest Jonathan, whose influence he feared. Consequently there would appear to have been a wholesale breakdown of law and order, and the Jewish population of the hellenistic towns

came under increasing pressure from their gentile neigh-
bours. Felix was replaced by Festus in 60 C.E. but without
any improvement in the overall situation, with the more
radical elements of the Jewish religion coming more and
more to the forefront; and the high priestly aristocracy, who
wanted to remain loyal to Rome for their own advantage,
were pushed unwillingly to the brink of revolt. It only took
a few more short years of weak procuratorial misrule to
fan the fire of open revolt that had been smouldering for
some time. The procuratorship of Florus (64-66) was the
climax. His insolence went beyond the bounds of his
predecessors, confiscating temple money and engaging
in open confrontation with the people of Jerusalem.
Despite the best efforts of Agrippa II to defuse the situation,
the Zealots, a party made up of Jewish priests of lesser
rank and country peasants, threw down the gauntlet to
Rome by taking control of the temple and refusing to allow
daily sacrifices on behalf of the Emperor. This was tantamount to an open declaration of war since the daily sacrifice
to their god was the Jewish equivalent to worship of the
Emperor, which was expected of every loyal inhabitant of
the empire as an act of civic duty.

There is no need here to detail the events of the ensuing
revolt. It is sufficient to know that after four years of blood-
shed and siege the Jerusalem temple was burned to the
ground by storming Roman troops, and a chapter of Jewish
history that had begun with the rebuilding of the temple by
the Babylonian exiles in 515 B.C.E. – the second temple
period, as Jewish historians call it – had come to an end.
The Arch of Titus in the Roman Forum still stands today
as a reminder of the historic event that was to have far-
reaching effects for Jews and Christians. The Jews fought
with courage, but, like all radical revolutionary movements
were bedeviled by internal party struggles and dissensions.
Josephus enumerates as many as six different groupings
in the revolutionary party, all deadly enemies of each other,
and to outline their differing ideologies here would be as

confusing as to attempt to explain the internal differences within the Irish revolutionary movement to an American who thinks the current unrest in Northern Ireland 'is a religious war'. The Roman general, Vespasian, who took control of the campaign (and after him his son Titus when the former had been declared Emperor in 69 C.E.), had only to play a wait-and-see game once the resistance in the countryside was broken. A few desperate revolutionaries held out at Masada, a desert fortress near the Dead Sea, until 73 C.E. before writing a glorious if macabre penultimate page to the Jewish resistance movement, by committing suicide rather than surrender to the Romans. Their heroism had little effect on the final settlement however. The land of Palestine was appropriated and given to loyal supporters of Rome, the whole province was now given Imperial rank, the tenth legion was stationed there and all Jews were forced to pay the half-shekel offering, formerly their annual contribution to the daily sacrifices, to the Capitoline Jupiter.

The suicides of Masada were a penultimate page because a final note had yet to be added. In 132 C.E. as the Roman Emperor, Hadrian, decided to build a temple to the Roman god Jupiter on the temple mount in Jerusalem, Jewish resistance broke out once more under a leader known to us only as Simeon Bar-Kochba, 'the Son of the Star'. The name presumably has messianic overtones based on the blessing of Balaam in the book of Numbers, which speaks of the future redeemer as 'a star that shall advance from Jacob' (Nm 24:16). Unfortunately, the second Jewish revolt did not have an historian comparable to Josephus whose seven books of the Jewish War is such a valuable chronicle of the first revolt. Our information on the extent of this revolt and its course is limited to a few general comments of later writers, and some recent archaeological finds in the Judaean desert. Apparently it was a bloody affair, confined mainly to the country, and the Jews were successful for a time before eventually their leaders were rounded up and executed, including Rabbi Aqiba, a leading teacher who had apparently given his blessing to the revolt and had acknowledged Bar-Kochba, as a messianic figure. The proposed temple was never built however, but the Judaism that survived this second purge was more than ever committed to 'another way', which made no claims to be political in any ordinary sense of the word. This development within Judaism beween the two revolts and its impact for emerging Christianity will be discussed in the next two chapters.

III. Rome and the Jews of the Diaspora

According to Strabo, a hellenistic geographer (+25 C.E. approx.) it was 'not easy to find a place in the inhabited world which this tribe (Jews) has not penetrated and which has not been occupied by it'. Certainly archaeological evidence of synagogues, cemeteries and other identifiably Jewish buildings are strewn across the length and breadth of the Roman Empire, and even beyond. While it is impossible to give any accurate estimate it seems certain that throughout our period the total Jewish population outside Palestine was far in excess of that in the homeland. Undoubtedly the social and economic opportunities that Hellenism afforded were largely responsible for this movement of Jews away from Palestine even though two centuries previously many souls in exile in Babylon had been pining to return there. Jews had left the homeland prior to Alexander's conquests, and many did not return from the Babylonian exile when the Persian Cyrus presented them with the opportunity to do so. Nevertheless, it is in hellenistic times that the greatest movement took place, and the legal arrangements that the Ptolemaic, Seleucid and later, the Roman administration arrived at in safeguarding their distinctive way of life was to have vital consequences for the first Christians also. One has only to consider Paul's missionary strategy as described in *Acts of the Apostles* - using Jewish synagogues as his first base of operation – to recognise how vital it was for the new movement to have certain structures established throughout the Roman world. To catalogue, not to speak of describing in any detail the history of the Jews at the various centres in the Graeco-Roman world, would take us far beyond the confines of this survey. We shall instead restrict ourselves to a number of more important questions with special relevance for our topic.

The fact that at the time of the first Jewish revolt against Rome we do not hear of any mass uprising throughout the empire, suggests that many Jews had a vested interest in not identifying with the revolutionaries in the fatherland. This is all the more significant in view of the fact that strong religious ties were maintained by means of the annual pilgrimages to the temple, the paying of the half-shekel offering for the daily sacrifices and the acceptance of various regulations on liturgical matters (e.g. dealing with the calendar) from the Jerusalem Sanhedrin. The only explanation must be that many Jews of the Diaspora had achieved a tolerable *modus vivendi* with the Roman authorities and were reluctant to disrupt such arrangements. Of course, this did not mean that these Jews did not suffer then and later, as popular feeling was aroused against them, especially in the cities of the eastern provinces adjacent to Palestine itself.

We are best informed about the status of Jews in Egypt and we may take it that the general outline was similar elsewhere, subject of course to local circumstances and at different periods. In Egypt we find Jews not merely playing a vital role in the life of the new city Alexandria, but also scattered in pockets throughout the countryside. The fact that a Jewish temple, set up by the expatriate Jewish high priest Onias IV (c. 170 B.C.E.), remained in existence until 73 C.E. is ample evidence of the extent to which differing Ptolemaic and later Roman authorities were prepared to go in granting both religious and legal status to Jews. Many of the Jews of the countryside were settlers to whom plots of land had been granted in reward for military services rendered, and which in time became hereditary. This was a common enough way of settling a particular area and ensuring its proper supervision under the hellenistic monarchies. The Jews had a reputation for military prowess, and it is no surprise to hear that the Seleucids also availed of their services. Thus we hear of Antiochus III (c. 210 B.C.E.) giving orders for 2,000 Jewish families from Mesopotamia to be resettled in the regions of Phrygia and Lydia (in Asia Minor) and promising them not just religious freedom, but various tax incentives also in return for their taking care of Seleucid interests in a troubled area.

Not all Jewish emigrants were so fortunate however, and the majority are to be found in the various cities of the empire. This explains why the question of citizenship looms so large in all the surviving documents, often giving rise to bitter recriminations between Jews and Gentiles. On this issue depended the rights and privileges of individuals and groups in regard to taxation, military service, trading and commerce, as well as other advantages in private and public life. However, citizenship of a particular city should not be confused with Roman citizenship as discussed earlier. The former was generally a necessary prerequisite for the latter, but even when this status was not achieved, it was still highly significant to have citizen's rights of Alexandria, Antioch or some other city, since the charters of the various cities were all ratified by the Emperor. *Some* Jews undoubtedly acquired citizen's rights of various cities, but evidence from Alexandria, Antioch, Asia Minor and other places suggests that attempts were made to achieve this status for *all* Jews. It would appear, however, that such attempts were unsuccessful, despite Josephus' suggestions to the contrary as part of his apologetic for his Roman readers. A letter from the Emperor Claudius to the citizens of Alexandria in the wake of civil disturbances there about the year 41 C.E. makes it clear that Rome was not prepared to authorise an upgrading of the Jewish legal status, and the same conclusion can be gleaned from documents relating to other cities also. Claudius writes:

> Wherefore, once again I conjure you that on the one hand the Alexandrians show themselves forbearing and kindly towards the Jews who for many years have dwelt in the same city, and *dishonour none of the rites observed by them in the worship of their god*, but allow them to observe their customs as in the time of the divine Augustus, which customs I also, after hearing both sides, have sanctioned; and on the other hand I explicitly order the Jews *not to agitate for more privileges than they formerly possessed*, and . . . not to force their way into gymnasiarchic or cosmetic games, while enjoying their own privileges and sharing a great abundance of advantages in a city not their own, and not to bring in or admit Jews who come down the river from Syria or Egypt, a proceeding that will compel me to conceive serious suspicions.

Claudius was clearly cognisant of the aspirations of the Alexandrian Jews but he was not prepared to allow any innovations, beyond the traditional freedom of religion and private association, and furthermore, he insisted that such rights could not be extended to other Jews from outside the city. How then are we to define the rights of the Jews in the various cities? In attempting to answer that question it is important to be aware that the charters of the various cities tolerated associations of people for different purposes: work, social purposes, religious, commercial and the like. Such toleration was all the more necessary in the hellenistic cities, over against those of classical Greece, because of the many different backgrounds and interests represented by the inhabitants of the cities in hellenistic times. Such associations were legally recognised even when their members did not possess full rights of citizenship. As an example of these diverse elements Strabo writes of the city of Cyrene (in North Africa): 'There were four classes in the city – citizens, farmers, resident aliens and Jews'. In all probability then, the legal status of Jewish communities within the cities was that of a free association for religious purposes, and this would also have included administration of the group's own internal affairs. This explains why we find fully organised quasi-autonomous Jewish communities with their own synagogues, officials and judicial system within the Greek cities, and also in Rome (cf. Ac 28:17). Inscriptions from various synagogues suggest a wide range of officials, both religious and saecular with different functions in regard to the life of the association. It would appear that at least in some instances there was a supervisory group of elders, headed by a leader, who formed the administrative body for several different synagogues within a particular city. In recognising early Christianity's indebtedness to Judaism one could easily overlook the community structures, legally recognised by the various city charters, that were ready to hand as models for Christian groups to organise themselves along similar lines.

Local circumstances, we have noted, determined to a large degree the toleration that such Jewish associations received at any particular time. Unlike the hellenistic monarchies that preceded them, the Romans appear to have attempted a universal policy towards the Jews in the various cities of the Empire. In all probability this policy had its origins in the treaty of friendship between the emerging Roman power in the East and Judas Maccabaeus (see opening citation of the chapter). Subsequently, Caesar, Mark Antony, Augustus and Claudius all made general appeals that the rights of the Jews 'to live according to their ancestral laws' be recognised. Yet at the same time, the treatment of the Jews in the city of Rome itself was a clear indication that toleration could not be presumed. As early as the year 139 B.C.E., that is within thirty years

of Judas' alliance of friendship and only a few years after
its renewal by his brother Simon, (1 Macc 14:24), we hear
that the *praetor* or official policeman in charge of foreigners,
expelled the Jews from Rome. In the extant account of the
incident astrologers are also mentioned as having been
banished. This is the first of many attempts that continued
on into imperial times to exclude foreign cults from Rome,
presumably because they were thought to be a threat to the
civic religion of the state, and in all probability it may
indicate that even at that early stage the Jews were attracting
many proselytes and others to their religion. By the middle
of the following century one may infer from Cicero's
remarks that the Roman Jewish community was large and
affluent in view of the gifts they had been able to send to
the Jerusalem temple. While Augustus made serious
attempts to curtail foreign cults in his efforts to restore
the old religion, it was under his successor, Tiberius, that
we hear of the next positive measures against Jews, but once
again Egyptian priests of the goddess Isis are included in the
expulsion orders. It is doubtful if all Jews actually left,
since in Caligula's reign twenty years later we hear of many
Jews in Rome at the time when the Emperor was pressing
to have his statue erected in the Jerusalem temple. While
Claudius apparently intended to reverse the harsh anti-
Jewish measures of his predecessor, his hand was forced
by rioting in which Jews were involved and so once again
we hear of an edict of expulsion, a fact recorded in *Acts of
the Apostles* also. It was this edict that brought Aquila
and Priscilla to Corinth, where they were to establish a
partnership with their fellow tent-maker, Paul, recently
arrived in the city (Ac 18:1-4).

Suetonius, a Roman writer of the second century, de-
cribes this particular expulsion as follows: 'Since the Jews
constantly make disturbances at the instigation of Chrestus,
he expelled them from Rome'. Many commentators see
this as a reference to Christ, and interpret Suetonius'
remarks to suggest that some Christian missionaries had

already appeared in the Jewish community in Rome preaching their version of the 'new religion', and that it was this that gave rise to the civil strife between them and more 'orthodox' Jews. This interpretation would find further confirmation if we could assume that Aquila and Priscilla were Christians before joining Paul at Corinth, something that the account in *Acts* at least suggests. Such a conclusion indicates that as far as Roman authorities were concerned Jews and Christians were still essentially one and the same movement coming out of Judaea. We do not know when exactly a visibly separate Christian church emerged in Rome, but certainly the *Epistle to the Romans* written about the year 56 C.E. seems to presuppose one that is no longer predominantly Jewish, and Paul's arrival in the city in the early sixties can only have accentuated the break. Certainly by the year 64 C.E. Roman Christians are a clearly recognisable group distinct from the Jews, though presumably sharing in the unpopularity of the latter with the Roman aristocracy, since Nero made them the scapegoats for the great fire, which had aroused the suspicion of the Roman populace against himself.

As we shall see in the final chapter, the Christians increasingly were to draw the special attraction of the Roman authorities, presumably because of their growing numerical strength throughout the Empire. Archaeological evidence in the city of Rome itself suggests that a very considerable Jewish population continued there, and this was not at all confined to any one quarter. At the same time aristocratic and influential Roman writers of the later first century C.E., like Seneca the philosopher, Martial the writer of epigrams, Juvenal the satirist, Quintilian the rhetorician and above all Tacitus the historian, betray a blatant anti-Jewish bias in their writing. Part of this can be attributed to their general contempt for things eastern and provincial. Tacitus disdainfully comments that all things hideous and shameful from every part of the world find their centre and become popular in Rome; and Juvenal, somewhat more colourfully but no less bitterly concurs: 'long ago the Syrian Orontes has poured its refuse into the Roman Tiber'. Yet while the Jews (and Christians) came in for their share of this general invective, there must have been special aspects of Judaism that classified it in Roman eyes as a 'superstition' – a derogatory term that contrasts with other respectable 'philosophies'. When their invective is examined it becomes clear that very often it consists of stock phrases, largely unexamined it would appear. The Jews are accused of shameful deeds, their origins were shameful and degenerate, they are given to idleness (the sabbath), and perhaps most important of all they pervert Roman religion and teach their converts contempt for family and fatherland. One might have expected that ideas like monotheism might have been of special interest to a philosopher/writer like Cicero who wrote a lengthy work on *The Nature of the Gods*, or that Jewish ethical ideas would have been attractive to a moral philosopher like Seneca. Yet there are no traces of any such interest on the part of the pagan writers.

It is difficult to assess the impact of such literature on popular as distinct from aristocratic attitudes towards Jews and Judaism. Some Jews certainly attained positions of honour in Roman circles, both administrative (Tiberius Alexander, the governor of Alexandria) and social (Herod Agrippa I in the Imperial court). But these appear to be the exceptions. Everywhere there is a synagogue we meet proselytes and God-fearers, that is those who had converted to Judaism or those who were attracted to certain aspects of the faith, but without undergoing circumcision as the formal rite of initiation for males. These must have been due, in part at least, to the active missionary activity of zealous Jews (cf. Mt 23:15), but also because of the search for a personal religion in the hellenistic and Roman world. It is equally difficult to estimate the value of such Jewish apologists as Josephus or Philo in explaining the meaning of Judaism and its history for interested outsiders. In all probability it was the daily living of the Jewish life that attracted most attention and comment, often no doubt favourable from those who had no axe to grind. The fact is that Judaism – with its stress on external practices of prayer, ritual purity, sabbath, circumcision, synagogue meetings for study of the sacred writings – had a high visibility by comparison with the occasional nature of the civic religions and the secret aspects of the Mysteries. Added to this were the very live contacts that were maintained between the Diaspora and the homeland in religious matters. The fact that the Jewish right to collect and send offerings with the pilgrims to the Jerusalem temple was maintained by imperial decree was not particularly popular with local magistrates, and there are cases of opposition and even of confiscation of the money. Nevertheless this aspect of the Jewish religion must have given it a very distinctive quality, even in the ancient world. Many from the Diaspora transferred to Jerusalem, a fact that is attested both by the presence of Greek-speaking synagogues and the presence of the so-called 'Hellenists' in the early Christian community there.

It might be expected that the Jewish religion would have been formally banned after the Palestinian Jews had dared to challenge the might of Rome in the two revolts. Yet the measures the Romans adopted, even in Palestine, were not that drastic. Within a relatively short space of time some official status was achieved by the schools of the rabbis, and eventually in the second century a single ruling head, officially styled the Patriarch, was recognised in law and had far-reaching administrative and judicial powers over Jews both at home and in the Diaspora. Clearly, the affronts that Rome had suffered, and the decisive, even ruthless suppression of the revolts did not impede the Roman imperial authorities from distinguishing between Jewish political aspirations which had to be suppressed in the name of Roman authority, and the religious aspirations which could be tolerated. Nor did the question of Emperor worship, which was as unacceptable to Jewish monotheism as it was to Christian beliefs about Jesus, change this official Roman policy. The loyal sacrifices offered on behalf of the Emperor to the Jewish God, and subsequently the half-shekel contribution, now devoted by Roman decree to the temple of Jupiter on the Capitol, must in time have eased the suspicions that Jews were anti-Roman and lacking in their civic duty. Besides, even when the Palestinian Jews had to bear the brunt of Roman wrath, a clear distinction was made in regard to Diaspora Jews. As he returned home in triumph after the destruction of the temple in 70 C.E. Titus refused the demand to dissolve the rights of the Jewish association in Antioch, thereby clearly indicating that the legal rights of the Diaspora Jews were on a different footing to those in Palestine. No doubt such official decisions did not increase the popularity of Jews within local communities, but it does illustrate how it was possible for Judaism to survive within the Empire, even when its political ambitions were thwarted. What Roman law guaranteed the Jews of the Diaspora was the right of free association, and given the nature of the Jewish religion this was adequate protection for it to survive.

This discussion of the status and social role of Jewish communities in the Diaspora is important not only in its own right, but also because of the light it sheds on early Christian life and activity within the Roman Empire of the first century. The journeys of Paul and other Christian missionaries throughout the Roman world, his collections for the 'poor in Jerusalem' (Ac 11:29-30; Rm 15:25-26; 2 Cor 9), the legal status of local Christian groups in Roman law and city charters, the organisation and internal structures of such groups – all of this becomes intelligible against the background of the Jewish Diaspora we have been discussing. Later we shall emphasise early Christianity's intellectual debt to this tradition. Here we wish to record its dependence on the visible and social role that Jews had been achieving for themselves within the Graeco-Roman world long before Christianity's arrival on the scene.

3. The Jewish Religion

3. THE JEWISH RELIGION

By the waters of Babylon, there we sat down and wept, when we remembered Zion (Ps 137:1).

Thus says Cyrus, King of Persia, "The Lord, the God of Heaven has given me all the kingdoms of the earth, and he has charged me to build him a house at Jerusalem which is in Judah. Whoever is among you of his people, may the Lord his God be with him. Let him go up." (2 Chron 36:23).

In those days lawless men came forth from Israel and misled many, saying: "Let us go and make a covenant with the Gentiles round about us, for since we separated ourselves from them many evils have come upon us" (1 Macc 1:11).

Then many who were seeking righteousness and justice went down to the wilderness to dwell there, they, their sons, their wives and their cattle, because evils pressed heavily upon them (1 Macc 2:29).

Our fathers worshipped on this mountain, and you say Jerusalem is the place where men ought to worship (Jn 4:20).

For the Pharisees and all the Jews do not eat unless they wash their hands, observing the tradition of the elders; and when they come from the market place they do not eat unless they purify themselves; and there are many other traditions they observe, the washing of cups and pots and vessels of bronze (Mk 7:3).

Now there was a man in Jerusalem whose name was Simeon, and this man was righteous and devout, looking for the consolation of Israel (Lk 2:25).

And he came to Nazareth where he was brought up; and he went to the synagogue, as his custom was, on the Sabbath day (Lk 4:16).

The Scribes and Pharisees sit on Moses' seat, so practice and observe whatever they tell you (Mt 23:2).

The Sadducees who say there is no resurrection came to him and they asked him a question (Mt 22:23).

From the days of John the Baptist until now the kingdom of heaven has suffered violence, and men of violence take it by force (Mt 11:12).

They are Israelites, and to them belong the sonship, the glory, the covenants, the giving of the law, the worship and the promises. To them belong the patriarchs, and of their race, according to the flesh, is the Christ. God who is over all be blessed forever. Amen (Rm 9:4-5).

THIS LAST quotation from St. Paul painfully highlights a fact that most Christians either do not know or do not care to acknowledge. I say 'painfully', because had Christianity's indebtedness to Judaism been recognised, centuries of slander and persecution climaxing in the atrocities of our times could have been avoided. It must frankly be admitted that many of the New Testament writings betray a sharp, polemical attitude towards Jews and Judaism, and unfortunately, once these texts are pried free of the historical context in which they were written they all too easily suggest that Judaism as a religion is outmoded, even degenerate. It is the aim of this chapter and the succeeding one to begin to set the record straight by attempting to capture something of the variety and complexity of Judaism in the first century of the Common Era, and at the same time to locate early Christianity, as a religious movement, within that spectrum. We have already outlined the external historical factors that the Jews encountered as part of the larger political worlds of Greece and Rome, and it will be necessary to recall these in this chapter also, since the history of the Jewish religion in our period can be seen as a response to those pressures, leading to the ultimate separation between the synagogue and the Christian church. By honestly confronting the facts of history, the polemics of the New Testament can hopefully be better understood, and need not act as a deterrent to Jews and Christians alike recognising their common heritage.

In speaking of Judaism as a religion it is important to distinguish between the Israelite religion as represented in the Old Testament (the Hebrew Scriptures for Jews) and Jewish beliefs and practices at the time of Jesus. While there is clearly a continuity between the two, much had happened in the centuries immediately prior to Christianity that was to be of decisive importance in indicating new directions for Jewish faith and practice. These developments were always grounded on the earlier religion of the Pentateuch and the Prophets, yet went considerably beyond those foundational documents in scope and intention. Central to the religious insights of the earlier period were the beliefs that Yahweh alone was the Lord of history, that he had chosen Israel as his own in a special way, and that he had revealed his will at Sinai in a set of moral imperatives that were absolutely binding if Israel wished to be faithful to her commitment as the chosen people. None of these central insights, and few of the practices and rituals through which they were expressed were ever lost sight of and are presupposed in our treatment, yet the Second Temple Period, as it is called, posed special problems and produced novel answers which will be our special focus in this chapter.

The Second Temple Period dates from the rededication of the restored Jerusalem temple in the year 515 B.C.E., and remote as it may seem, this is the more correct starting point for a discussion of Judaism than the more usual one of Alexander's conquests, two centuries later. Of course the latter was the beginning of a new and very different epoch in the religious history of the whole Mediterranean world, as outlined in our first chapter, and it is not surprising to find developments within Judaism parallel to those taking place on the larger scene. Nevertheless, the experience of the Babylonian exile two centuries earlier and its immediate afermath had in a sense prepared Judaism for the crisis that Hellenism was to bring on, and so it is to these earlier developments that we must first turn our attention (I). Subsequently we shall treat in turn of the hellenistic reform and its repercussions within Judaism (II); the 'Four Philosophies' and their beliefs (III); and the rise of rabbinic Judaism in the Jamnia period (IV).

I. The Exile and the Return

Ps 137 (first citation), aptly described as 'the ballad of the exiles' in the *Jerusalem Bible*, poignantly expressed the trauma to Israel's faith that the exile caused. The belief that Yahweh was the Lord of History, which had been so central to early Israel's religious experience (cf. for example, Dt 26:5-11; Jos 24) had suffered a severe setback in 587 B.C.E. In that year the Babylonians finally destroyed the Jerusalem temple and deported some of the leaders of the Jerusalem religious society, including the king, the officials of the temple, and other members of the aristocracy, leaving behind 'the poorest of the land to be vinedressers and ploughmen' (2 Kgs 25:12). The promise made to David that his son should sit on his throne forever (2 Sm 7) seemed now like an empty wish, and the belief that Yahweh had made his name to dwell in the Jerusalem temple, so recently reaffirmed in the Deuteronomic reform (cf. Dt 12:11) had suffered a rude shock. The prophet Ezechiel, possibly addressing the exilic community, yet reflecting his own sorrow as a temple priest, writes of his vision which saw the glory of Yahweh hovering over the city before departing to the East (Ez 11:22f). And the same prophet suggests that there were some in Israel who even queried whether or not God was just (Ez 18:25).

Yet disappointment, dismay and disillusionment were not the only reactions of the Jewish community in exile. Clearly some practical arrangements and adaptations had to be made if all was not to be lost, especially as there are hints that the exiled King of Judah, Jehoiachin, was honourably received at the Babylonian court. In such circumstances total absorption into the local environment would have been very easy, yet clearly, some at least of the more devout exiles were able to see beyond the externals and detect within the tragedy the deeper plan of God. Even prior to the exile, the prophet Jeremiah had prepared for the seeming rejection by warning that Yahweh's ties with Jerusalem were not irrevocable in face of a wicked people. Ezechiel, his younger contemporary, and later, the anonymous author of Is 40-55 encouraged the exiles to a new awareness of themselves as the true remnant of Israel whose sufferings could be redemptive for all (Ez 11:15-21; Is 53). Probably the impetus for such a reorganisation came from the priests and Levites, whose social standing in Babylonia would have counted for nothing and who would have considered themselves the guardians of Israel's religious heritage in the absence of the temple. No doubt it was in these same circles that the decree of Cyrus, allowing Jews to return, found its most enthusiastic response, and so those who eventually returned to Jerusalem would be doing so for very definite religious reasons that were to mark them off within the restored community.

First, however, we must briefly consider the experience of the exile itself and attempt to assess its impact on religious views. The first and most important effect of the experience was to create a greater awareness of Israel's past inheritance and traditions, and the putting of these into writing. It is sometimes said that the first two parts of the Hebrew Scriptures (the Law and the Prophets – the Writings are the third division) were more or less finalised in this period. However, that is an oversimplification, given the fact that both sections went through considerable adaptation in the subsequent period as they were interpreted to meet the various crises of the restored community's life. Nevertheless, there is no denying that the exile was an important, indeed decisive moment in the collection of the traditions of the earlier period. This was a very natural reaction to the crisis, since without the temple there was no tangible sign of Israel's special identity. Collecting the traditions of the past was a most natural way of filling that vacuum. Henceforth, all development within Jewish life would be made with reference to this body of traditions, and their study would give rise to a new class of scholars, the scribes, in the succeeding centuries. Closely related to this development was the emergence of the synagogue as an important institution in Jewish life. Originally, this Greek word and its Jewish equivalent signified a meeting for any purpose, but as early as the exile it apparently had acquired religious overtones, perhaps primarily as an act (rather than a place) of meeting for prayer and the collection and study of the sacred traditions. Already then in this exilic situation, deprived of the temple, one can detect the beginning of alternative institutions that were eventually to replace the temple as the centre of Jewish life and worship. To be sure, as an institution the synagogue in Babylonia was probably highly unstructured and *ad hoc*, but the important fact remains that Judaism was able to find an alternative way of worshipping its God when deprived of the temple. This discovery was to stand it in good stead in the succeeding centuries.

We have already mentioned the impact that the exile had had on the faith of Israel, even to the point of raising a serious question concerning the nature of God and the divine/human relationship as Israel had experienced it. These questions were to find different expressions in the post-exilic period where differing trends of thought are readily recognisable in the variety of literary productions during this period, as distinct from the relatively homogeneous narrative, legal and prophetic-oracular material of earlier times. In particular Wisdom and Apocalyptic emerge as two new and dominant literary trends. And while they were certainly to blend in the melting pot of the religious and cultural upheaval of the succeeding centuries they had each originally very different origins and addressed rather different questions. As already mentioned, the loss of king and homeland had given rise to serious problems about the action of God in history, problems that became more intensified for the zealous upholders of Israel's traditions on the return. Besides, the swings in the political pendulum of power – from Babylonian, to Persian, to Greek, to Ptolemaic, to Seleucid, to Roman – all kept alive the questions of the divine purpose on the historical and cosmic planes, and it was to such problems as these that Apocalyptic addressed itself, especially when such shifts affected certain segments of the restored community, as we shall see more clearly in the next section. On the other hand, traditional wisdom, such as one finds in *The Book of Proverbs*, is now pressed into service of the more everyday questions of life and death. While Wisdom's court origins had provoked the criticism of the prophets before the exile as being saecular and lacking in proper trust in Yahweh's lordship (Is 29:14), it can be put to use in a more highly individualistic age (cf. for example Ez 17) where now each man's personal lot has to be discovered and lived out, often in face of the dumb opaqueness of life's experiences (cf. for example, *Qoheleth* and *Job*). Once again we must move well beyond the immediate exilic experience before problems like these are fully articulated and addressed. Yet there is little difficulty in tracing their origins at least in part to the Babylonian experience.

Our lack of real historical sources makes it difficult to trace the religious history of the restored community in any great detail. However, a number of trends and issues can be detected from the first fifty years or so which are also present when again the sources become adequate almost three centuries later. This suggests that the earlier tensions continued to dominate, with of course the added complicating factor of Hellenism, as we shall see. Basically, the tension was now one of deciding who were the more faithful interpreters of Israel's religious traditions. At least in the first century after the return, two opposing groups emerge – the returnees on the one hand, variously called 'the men of the exile', 'the holy race', 'Israelites', and on the other, the natives who had not experienced the exile, usually opprobriously styled 'the people of the land' in the sources (The Books of *Ezra* and *Nehemiah* as well as the prophets *Third Isaiah* (56-66), *Haggai, Zechariah* and *Malachi*) all of which are definitely written from the perspective of the former group. The issues between these groups (and various subgroups on both sides) were varied; marriage with foreigners, the observance of the purity laws, relations with the Samaritans who had opposed the rebuilding of the Jerusalem temple, forms of sacrificial worship. Yet all of these have to do with the question of the self-identity of the community, and clearly the returning exiles were determined that the only way for Judaism to retain its distinctiveness was by a policy of rigid separatism, no doubt based on the experience of what had happened to their more open minded co-religionists in exile. The missions of Ezra, the scribe, and later Nehemiah, are concerned with this question of the separation of the community from outside contacts, especially in the area of mixed marriages (cf. Ezra 10:1-44; Neh 9:2; 10:29-31). The necessity for such reforms suggests that the returnees had not been totally successful in imposing their point of view, and we hear from Josephus that later this issue split the Jerusalem community, causing some dissident priests to join the Samaritans and assist in the building of the rival temple on Mt. Gerizim. Clearly, not even the towering figure of Ezra, a second Moses, was able to eliminate the opposing point of view.

These conflicts, which can only be referred to here in passing, are of great significance for understanding subsequent divisions and struggles within Judaism, something we shall see in greater detail in section III, below. Their importance for our purposes is the fact that they suggest very different, even rival claims to what is normative Judaism, if we may use that term for this period. Even though the monarchy was divided in earlier times between north and south, there never was a division on the basis of religious beliefs, at least not to the point where one group considered itself to be the sole authentic voice of the communal religious experience. Clearly then, the exile has introduced a new and very different element into Judaism, radicalising it into various conflicting factions, and from this perspective the encounter with Hellenism is only another phase of an ongoing problem. Yet, strangely, despite the efforts of the rigorists to separate themselves entirely from outside influences, it would appear that they were less than fully successful. In the very body of literature that is generally considered to emanate from their circles, Apocalyptic, one finds traces of what today are generally regarded by scholars to be Persian influences: belief in angels and demons, a dualistic understanding of the world, concern with the stars and other heavenly bodies, to be seen in the special interest in calendars. It would appear that no matter how seriously one takes the notion of religious separation and isolation from the larger cultural world, this cannot be effectively realised when other factors, cultural, economic and political are ranged against it. We must now turn to a new phase of Judaism's struggle with this problem in terms of the hellenistic reform of 167 B.C.E.

II. The Hellenistic Reform and its Repercussions within Judaism

In our opening chapter we discussed some of the cultural and economic results of Hellenism, and we also saw the way in which these developments posed a real challenge to the established religions. Corresponding to the one-culture world of which all were becoming increasingly conscious, we find that the notion of one god (of whom local gods were mere manifestations) was also becoming more acceptable. It causes little surprise then to discover that those Jews who had been affected by the general movement of Hellenism shared some of these assumptions and were ready to identify Yahweh with Zeus, 'for since we separated ourselves from them (the gentiles) many evils have come upon us', as the laconic citation from 1 Macc (third quotation above) put it. The evils of separation were undoubtedly social and economic, and so the pattern and tensions we have already seen in the exilic community and that of the immediate return repeat themselves. But who were these 'lawless men' and what was the background to their free-thinking attitudes within Judaism?

There is fairly general agreement that throughout the third century B.C.E. – the 'hidden century', because of our lack of sources – there had developed within Palestinian Judaism a lay nobility side by side with the priestly aristocracy who, technically at least, were the sole rulers in the temple state. Two families appear in our scattered sources, the Tobiads, as representative of the former, and the Oniads, of the latter. Naturally there was rivalry that came to a head when the Ptolemaic king, as overlord of Palestine, made a Tobiad the chief of the Jews, with the right to collect the taxes. What had effectively taken place was a separation of church and state, to use a modern phrase, and even though the highpriesthood was reaffirmed in its position of primacy on the Seleucid takeover of Palestine, the hellenised aristocracy had discovered that control of the highest religious office meant control of the Jewish state and its policies. Consequently they availed of the first opportunity to seize power, which occurred because of the financial straits of the young Seleucid king, Antiochus IV, (known as Epiphanes, because of his desire to be considered a divine being). First Jason (the brother of the existing high priest) and then Menelaus (who was not even of priestly stock) were installed and it seemed as though the hellenisers would have their way. Jerusalem was to be turned into a Greek city, thus abrogating its charter as head of a temple state, and an even more damaging innovation was the introduction of a Greek school where young Jewish boys were to learn the Greek way of life and even abandon circumcision, the sign of the Jewish male (2 Macc 4:7-9). Resistance mounted, probably from the *hasîdîm*, or pious ones, whose background and views we will presently discuss, but when Antiochus had his military hopes thwarted in Egypt, he invaded the Jerusalem temple carrying off some of its treasures and subsequently sent a general to impose on the Jews also a decree that his whole kingdom should worship the one god. This was followed by a wholesale religious persecution that lasted for over three years, until at last a family of country priests, the Maccabees, launched a resistance movement. This eventually led to the repeal of the hated decree and the rededication of the Jerusalem temple, giving rise to the feast of Hanukkah, or Dedication feast that we find Jesus observing according to Jn 10:17.

The resistance movement brought together various elements within Jewish society, but once the hour of crisis had passed it soon became apparent that there were serious differences between them as to what constituted the national ideal. The extreme hellenisers who had been prepared to identify Yahweh with Zeus found that they were a tiny minority, and with the death of Menelaus, their representative in the highpriesthood, there was never any likelihood of their succeeding even with the active support of the Seleucid king. One little episode is perhaps indicative of the temporising with Hellenism that was current. On the occasion of the games in honour of the god Hercules at Tyre, Jason the incumbent high priest had sent an offering on behalf of the god, but the envoys decided that the sacred money should not be spent in this manner and put it to another use (2 Macc 4:18-20). Thus, the extreme hellenisers could hardly expect to dismantle the Jewish religion entirely – an interesting contrast with the Samaritans at Mount Gerizim where the cult of Zeus was actively fostered (2 Macc 6:2). Yet this did not mean that all hellenistic tendencies were purged from the Jerusalem aristocracy. The high priest appointed by the Seleucids after the rededication of the temple, Alcimus, is typical of the modified hellenisers now emerging. Yet once the temple scribes had ascertained that he was of the priestly line he was accepted, even by the *hasîdîm* (1 Macc 7:12f).

The Maccabaean brothers, Judas, Jonathan and Simon, appear to have adopted a middle position between the hellenisers and the *hasîdîm* once the immediate threat of the reform was over. While the authors of the books of Maccabees treat them as national heroes who were ready to sacrifice all for faith and fatherland, the political sequel indicates that their intentions were not just religious. Thus in the year 152 B.C.E. Jonathan accepted the office of high priest from the Seleucid monarch of the day (1 Macc 10:21), even though he was not of the house of Sadok, the high priestly family, and this led to a radical reaction on the part of some Jews, as we shall see. Subsequently Simon, the third brother, also accepted the office, thereby continuing the precedent that the civil ruler in the newly emerging Hasmonaean state should also be the religious leader (1 Macc

14:41). Thus we have the anomaly that the family who were celebrated as the saviours of the Jewish faith at the moment of crisis became, themselves, the champions of a thoroughly hellenistic state retaining control of religious affairs at the same time. It is in reaction to this group that, as we shall see in the next section, the Pharisees emerge for the first time as the party of opposition.

A third grouping mentioned in our sources for the period are the *hasîdîm* (literally 'the pious ones'), whom we have mentioned more than once. We first hear of the one group of *hasîdîm* (called literally a 'synagogue', suggesting groups or conventicles) who joined forces with the Maccabees in the struggle for the law. They are described as 'mighty warriors of Israel' (1 Macc 2:42), and were obviously in the forefront of the resistance movement, not pacifists, as is sometimes supposed on the basis of an earlier passage in the same chapter where we read of a group 'who were seeking righteousness and justice', and who had gone to the desert, and left themselves undefended on the Sabbath (1 Macc 2:29-38). As we shall see, there may have been connections between these groups, but at least on the author's presentation they are not identical. When next we hear of the *hasîdîm* they are accompanied by scribes enquiring into the pedigree of the proposed high priest of the restoration, Alcimus, and on being satisfied as to his legitimacy, they were the first to seek peace (1 Macc 7:12f). This seems to be the point at which they and the Maccabees parted company: the former were content to give up the struggle for independence once they were assured freedom to practice their religious beliefs, whereas the latter were determined that nothing short of national independence was adequate, even if this meant compromising with 'the enemy'.

On the basis of these scanty references it might appear that little can be said of the *hasîdîm* or their distinctive background and point of view. However, it is probable that their role in the resistance was much greater than the author of 1 Macc allows, writing as he was in support of the Maccabees who were under attack because of their conduct of affairs in the Hasmonaean state. It is usual to attribute the book of Daniel to the *hasîdîm* for there we can detect attitudes which are more akin to their view of the crisis, than the more nationalistic minded Maccabees, who in fact do not feature very prominently in Dn (cf. the reference to 'a little help' at 11:34). The real heroes of this book, clearly written under the stress of the persecution of Antiochus, are 'the wise', who understand God's mysterious plan (12:10), have not shirked from giving their lives for their beliefs (11:23-25) and hope for ultimate vindication (12:2-3). They are 'the saints of the Most High' who are to inherit the kingdom given to the Son of Man, who, at least in this work, stands as a corporate image for the whole group (7:13.23). Their sanctity finds its model in Daniel, as he is described in chapters 1-6; he is a strict observer of the dietary laws, remains steadfast in his Jewish faith despite threats, is endowed with the spirit of God and can interpret hidden mysteries. In a word, the *hasîdîm* are the group among whom an apocalyptic vision of Israel's destiny has been fostered, and this pre-dates the immediate crisis which produced the book of Daniel. Indeed it could be argued that these are the very groups we have already met in the immediate post-exilic community, imbued with a deep sense of God's purposes in history and among whom the voices of the prophets of the past were brought to life by being constantly reinterpreted to address new crises, real or perceived by the group within the larger community.

As already mentioned, Apocalyptic, both as a mode of structuring reality and as a literary form, is a particular development of this period, with special relevance for early Christianity, as we shall see. There are a number of characteristic features of the apocalyptic mentality, if we may so call it, that are worth discussing, however briefly. To begin with, apocalyptic is the outgrowth of the belief that Yahweh is Lord of History, but now this belief is transferred to the cosmic plane, and the present time is conceived of as being abandoned to the powers of evil, soon to be superseded by a new age where the just will be rewarded and evil in whatever form destroyed. This doctrine of 'the two ages', as it is called, finds poetic expression in a first century Apocalypse, the *Fourth Book of Ezra*: 'For the world has lost its youth. The times begin to wax old . . . For this cause the Most High has made not one age but two ages'. The doctrine finds more concrete expression in other writings also. Thus in the Mishnah (the Jewish law code) we find an enumeration of all those to be excluded from the world to come (*Sanhedrin* 10:1), and in the gospel of *Mark*, we read that those who have followed Jesus are to have an hundredfold in this world and in the world to come everlasting life (Mk 10:30). Thus the doctrine of the two ages is the theological underpinning for the belief in the idea of resurrection of the dead – a doctrine that finds its first unequivocal expression in the book of Daniel: 'and many of those who sleep in the dust of the earth shall awake, some to everlasting life, and some to shame and everlasting contempt. And those who are wise shall shine like the brightness of the firmament' (Dn 12:2-3). Apocalyptic then provided the conceptual and symbolic framework for the first Christians to express their conviction and experience of Jesus' vindication by God. As Paul puts it rather forcefully: 'if there is no resurrection from the dead, then Christ has not been raised' (1 Cor 15:13). This latter occurrence is a particular, indeed unique instance of a firmly held belief of wider range and application.

There are other aspects of the apocalyptic view of the world that found a congenial context within early Christianity. Of first importance is the notion of the kingdom of God. This idea, which of course had its origins in the covenant notion in early Israel and found concrete expression in the Davidic monarchy, is transferred to the coming age in the apocalyptic view. It stands over against the kingdoms of this age (in Daniel, the Persians, Alexander, Ptolemies and Seleucids; in later Apocalypses, the Romans), who are seen as the embodiment of the evil forces oppressing the wise or the just, as the addressees are variously called. The establishing of God's rule is not a purely spiritual event however, but encompasses a new world, where God's purposes for history can be truly established. Thus, the dualism (good and evil forces ranged against each other) that is often seen as a distinguishing feature of apocalyptic is not as pessimistic as is sometimes imagined. There is no necessary flight from the world as evil, nor is the physical universe, including the human body, perceived as essentially corrupt, as in gnosticism. Rather the hope of the new world to come is the source of inspiration for the just to live out their radical understanding of God's will in the present.

Closely associated with the notion of the Kingdom of God is the figure of the Son of Man. Though much has been written about the background and origin of this figure, for our purposes all that is required is to acknowledge that the figure is central to the coming age, either as the representative of the whole community of the just as in *Daniel* (7:13.23), or as their judge and vindicator in the *Book of Enoch*, a collection of apocalyptic material that at least in its older strata pre-dates Christianity. It is worth quoting a few scattered lines from this composite work as an indication not merely of the thematic, but even the verbal links with the gospels:

> In that hour the Son of Man was named
> In the presence of the Lord of Spirits . . .
> He shall be a staff to the righteous whereon to
>   stay themselves and not fall.
> And he shall be a light of the Gentiles,
> And the hope of those who are troubled in heart . . .
> And there was great joy among them (the blessed)
> Because the name of that Son of Man had been
>   revealed to them,
> And he sat on the throne of his glory,
> And the sum of judgement was given to the Son of Man,
> And he caused the sinners to pass away and be destroyed
>   from off the face of the earth.

By contrast with the reference in *Daniel*, the figure has clearly become an individual who functions as an end-time saviour for the just in the apocalyptic struggle that is thought of as about to break into the present evil situation. There is no systematic linking of this figure with the more traditional conceptions of the Messiah, as these had been worked out in relation to earlier texts, yet one can detect a general tendency to colour the picture of the one with features from the others. Perhaps the two most significant current images of the Messiah were those of the Davidic ruler (based on 2 Sm 7), and the prophet like Moses (Dt 18:18). Given the political situation of the Jewish community it was natural to see the former as a figure of national liberation, the ideal king, who would not only be victorious over Israel's enemies, but would also be a just and righteous king. He would thus be a striking contrast to the Hasmonaean and Herodian kings whose policies and values were so alien to the ideals of the *hasidim*, as these had been developed and carried forward by the various parties into the first century. The other image of the Messiah that had wide currency among various groups, including the early Christians, was that of the 'prophet like Moses'. To this figure was attributed the idea of end-time revealer, or definitive interpreter of the law for the group in question. Here the emphasis is not only on knowledge of when the apocalyptic drama would unfold, but also how the just should conduct themselves in the period of trial and struggle that was to immediately precede the new age. These two examples of messianic images and their colouring with traits of the Son of Man figure of the apocalyptists, should help to illustrate just how fluid a figure the Messiah was in Judaism of the first century. Sometimes the question about Jesus as Messiah is posed by Christians, as though there was one fixed and immutable conception, shared by all elements of the people. The pervasiveness of apocalyptic ideas, even outside the circles of the *hasidim*, and their wider dissemination through the various groups, ensured that there could be no *one* Messiah image shared by all. By its very nature apocalyptic deals in symbols and metaphors that are evocative rather than descriptive, and thus capable of multiple applications depending on the point of view of those interpreting them.

This brings us to a final feature of Apocalyptic which has been receiving increased attention in recent studies, namely its social background. What is the social situation of the groups among whom Apocalyptic thrives, and what light would an answer to that question shed on the *hasidim*, and those who were heirs to their views subsequently, including the early Christians? Earlier studies had suggested that Apocalyptic originated and was most at home among the destitute classes, who substituted another world for the one filled with misery and despair which was their present lot. However, the intellectual sophistication demanded in decoding the highly elaborate symbolism of apocalyptic literature suggests a more intellectual ethos. Anthropological studies would seem to confirm this, in that they suggest the true home of Apocalyptic to be among the relatively, not the absolutely deprived. Relative deprivation focuses not so much on material conditions as on the exclusion from power and prestige within a larger society. The relatively deprived aspire to controlling the institutions of power, but are excluded from doing so, and consequently feel alienated and deprived. By way of compensation they reconstruct another view of reality, another story, if you will, of how things really are, according to which it is they who control the instruments of power, and their version of life and its meaning becomes the dominant one. Such an understanding of the social matrix of Apocalyptic would enormously enhance our understanding of early Jewish apocalyptic literature and the circles within which it was produced. For one thing it would explain the nature of apocalyptic language, the rigidity of its views and the contempt that it shows, not only for the external enemy, but for those within the larger group who are perceived as showing less than a solid front against the recognised source of evil. It would also explain how the ideals of the *hasidim* were to be carried forward and fostered by those who felt alienated from the temple and its cult within a theocratic state. As the Maccabees and their successors astutely perceived, in a state whose *raison d'etre* was religious, it was necessary for those wielding saecular power also to control the source of religious power, and that meant the temple, its priesthood and cult. This explains why they and the *hasĩdĩm*, whose devotion to the religious traditions of Israel appeared to give them special authority as its interpreters, were to reach the parting of the ways. The subsequent stages of that parting are best told in terms of the Jewish parties that Josephus describes for us, and of which we know from other sources also, and this is the subject of our next section.

III. *The Religious Parties in First Century Judaism*

In describing the various groups within first century Judaism, Josephus consciously calls them 'philosophies', presumably in the hope of making Judaism appear both reasonable and attractive to outsiders, who were often made to think of it, as well as of other eastern cults as 'superstitions' and therefore unworthy of Roman *gravitas*. He even likens the different Jewish groups to the better known Graeco-Roman ones: Pharisees and Stoics; Sadducees and Epicureans; Essenes and Cynics. At first sight this might appear to be a clever ploy by the ex-general turned apologist, yet lacking substance. However, on closer examination, there is more than a little plausibility to the comparison. As we shall see, all the Jewish parties were in a sense the outgrowth of Judaism's response to the extreme threat of Hellenism at the time of the hellenistic reform, and its subsequent having to come to terms with a more modified, but no less vital form, mediated through the Roman world. In a real sense then all branches of Judaism in this period are a response to the larger ethos we have been examining. In our first chapter we saw that the various trends in Graeco-Roman religion and philosophy were equally a reponse to that larger world and the problems that it posed. Viewed in this light there is nothing improbable in finding developments in Graeco-Roman religion paralleled within Judaism in this period also, and the comparisons may prove to be illuminating as we examine each of the parties and their philosophies. We must always keep in mind that despite their differences, they were all thoroughly Jewish, each claiming that it rather than the others was the definitive interpreter of Jewish tradition, and so the authentic voice of God for his people.

(i) THE SADDUCEES

'The Sadducees, the second of the orders, do away with Fate altogether, and remove God beyond, not merely the commission, but the very sight of evil. They maintain that a man has the free choice of good and evil, and that it rests with each man's will whether he follows the one or the other. As for the persistence of the soul after death, penalties in the underworld, and rewards, they will have none of them'.

This is just one of the descriptions of the Sadducees that Josephus gives us, which, with its mention of Fate and the discussion of free will, is clearly couched in language that would be familiar to the intelligent Roman reader. In fact neither Fate nor free will were ever central questions within Judaism, where the notion of God's election and care for his people, and their free response as the chosen people, made such theoretic questions rather irrelevant. Nevertheless, it is significant that the Sadducees' disbelief in the idea of an after-life as mentioned by Josephus corresponds with one of the few other direct pieces of information we have about them, coming from the New Testament where we also hear of their rejection of the idea of resurrection from the dead (Mk 12:18-23; Ac 23:6). This is all the more significant in view of the fact that there are no extant writings of the Sadducees, and we must attempt to briefly reconstruct their history and beliefs on the basis of data that comes from their known critics.

There is fairly general agreement that the name Sadducee comes from the priest Sadok, whom Solomon appointed to take charge of the ark of the covenant on his accession to power in Jerusalem (1 Kgs 2:35), and in a later writing, the sons of Sadok are described as being the legitimate line of priests for the restored temple (Ez 40:46; 43:19; 44:15; 48:11). It is noteworthy that if this is the correct derivation of their name, it was also appropriated by some branches of the Essenes, as we learn from one of their documents. Clearly the question of who the legitimate priests were was a very central one in first century Judaism, and this has a very real bearing on our discussion of the sociological basis for these different groupings.

The Sadducees are mentioned for the first time in our sources by Josephus, during the reign of John Hyrcanus, where it is clear that they and the Pharisees disagree on certain questions of Jewish practice. The Pharisees object to the king's right to be high priest, who thereupon sided with the Sadducees, and from this we may infer that they had no objection to the Hasmonaean take-over of the highpriesthood. With this insight into the Sadducees' position on such a central issue we can fairly assume that as a party they must have organised within the hellenised aristocracy associated with the highpriesthood, in the immediate restoration period. Certainly that was their social position in the New Testament, and it probably had remained constant, especially since Josephus tells us that they were not very popular, and had little success with the people as a whole. Given this background, then, they were at the opposite extreme to the *hasidim* at the time of the restoration. Unlike the latter, their political and social interests were greater than their ideological convictions, and so they accepted whoever was the incumbent high priest, be it Alcimus, Jonathan or John Hyrcanus, probably arrogating for themselves the grandiose title as a way of legitimating their position within the community as a whole.

With this understanding of their social position, it is easy to grasp the theological 'conservatism' of the Sadducees. Josephus tells us that they rejected any law that was not based on Scripture, and, as we shall see, this together with their denial of the afterlife really differentiated them from the Pharisees. The law codes of the Pentateuch with their legislation for the temple state and the special role of the priesthood, were clearly a suitable charter for the Sadducees and their position within Jewish society. The formal religion of the cult, which they or their henchmen controlled, was an adequate expression of their piety. It mattered little to them that such a religion did nothing to meet the needs of the large Jewish population living in the Diaspora, far removed from temple and cult and in danger of being submerged by the culture of the hellenistic cities. Probably some Sadducees were large landowners, living indeed in Jerusalem, but drawing the benefits from a peasantry whose religious beliefs committed them to a tithing of the produce of the land for the upkeep of their clergy. Thus a Sadducaean landowner who happened to be a priest stood to profit doubly from his land by receiving both the religious dues (payable in part to the local priest) and the rent for leasing or other rights granted to the peasants.

In such a situation of social and economic superiority one can readily recognise the Sadducees' lack of interest in novelty or change and their resentment of those who might propose it. Here perhaps lies the explanation of the curious fact that though the gospels relate many debates between Jesus and the Pharisees at various stages of the ministry, the Sadducees (in the persons of the chief priests and elders) are the dominant anti-figures of the last trial. The religion of Jesus could be seen as an attack on temple religion as that was controlled by the Sadducees. Understood as a 'holy man', a figure of great social as well as religious significance in the ancient world, divine power was accessible in him outside the normal channels, and that was to challenge the very necessity of the elaborate ritual system of the temple religion. The author of the Fourth Gospel has shrewdly recognised the significance of this threat of Jesus to the Jewish establishment by having the high priest express his anxieties as follows: 'What are we to do? For this man performs many signs. If we let him go on thus, everyone will believe in him, and the Romans will come and destroy both our (holy) place and our nation' (Jn 11:48). In his eyes destruction of the holy place was tantamount to destruction of the nation, a supposition not shared by the Pharisees. Besides, the Romans had officially tolerated a temple religion in which sacrifices on behalf of the Emperor were offered to the God of the Jews. Were a popular religious movement to be generated around Jesus not only would the position of social supremacy of the Sadducees be challenged, but the ire of the Romans against all Jews would be aroused.

The other point of Sadducaean doctrine on which we are well informed is their denial of an after-life. As we have seen it was from the circles of the *hasîdîm* that this belief emanated, in response to a faith in God, the vindicator of the just, that was challenged by the severe religious persecution of the times. If our assumption that the Sadducees originated within the hellenistic circles is correct and our assessment of their social situation accurate, the question of an after-life would not have posed itself in such stark terms for them. In accepting some at least of the views of the hellenistic outlook they would more easily have been able to adapt their faith to the times, thereby avoiding confrontation and persecution. Consequently, the question of reward for fidelity in the face of persecution did not arise. Their continued dominance of the economic and social life in the emerging Hasmonaean state meant that the old Israelite belief grounded in the Pentateuch, that the good prosper and the wicked are punished, was quite

adequate to justify in religious terms their own present
dominance, without any need to pose the question of the
future in a serious way.

It is interesting to examine their confrontation with
Jesus on this issue against this background (Mk 12:18-23).
The passage is a classic example of the differing appeals
to the tradition of the law of Moses made by the different
religious points of view within Judaism. The Sadducees
seek to reduce the notion of resurrection to an absurdity
by citing the example of the levirate law, whereby a man
is obliged to raise up children to his dead brother on the
basis of Deut 25:5, and the case cited would appear to create
insurmountable legal problems in the world to come. Jesus'
reply claims in effect that the Sadducees are fundamen-
talists: they do not understand the power of God and so they
have an extremely literal understanding and application of
the scripture text, but they are in error. Jesus then cites
another text from 'Moses', that is from the Exodus tradition
about Yahweh's appearance to Moses, and not from *Daniel*,
the only clear literal reference to resurrection, as we have
seen. The text cited, 'I am the God of Abraham, the God of
Isaac and the God of Jacob', scarcely contains the notion
on a purely literalist interpretation, yet one can readily
recognise how somebody like Jesus or the Pharisees, who
have accepted the notion on the other grounds, could read
it into such a text as Ex 3:6, or perhaps, better, 'draw it out'
of the text. Yet the ploy of staying with Moses, not citing
from a book (*Daniel*) whose authority the Sadducees would
probably not have accepted, was very much part of the style
of argument that was current at the time, and which is so
frequently documented in the Talmudic literature. What is
noteworthy in this case is that both Jesus and Pharisaic
scribes not merely believed in the same doctrine but would
have employed very similar exegetical tactics in refuting
an opponent.

At the outset we mentioned Josephus' likening of the
Sadducees to the Epicureans. Clearly the comparison does

not hold up under strict scrutiny. Yet it is noteworthy that for both, the idea of an after-life was neither necessary nor acceptable. It is probably unfair to describe the Epicureans as atheists, but they certainly saw the gods as far removed from the sphere of man, living in epicurean bliss. In this regard their doctrine of God and that of the Sadducees are not dissimilar. By confining the divine presence to the temple and the cult, God was indeed removed beyond 'not merely the commission but the sight of evil', to use Josephus' phrase, that is, from the sphere of the everyday. A frozen tradition from the past, rather than a living and self-renewing one, was clearly more in keeping with such a God concept.

(ii) THE ESSENES

At the very opposite end (from the Sadducees) in the spectrum of Jewish parties were the Essenes, who are not mentioned at all in the New Testament. Nevertheless since the discovery of the Dead Sea Scrolls in 1947 – which are almost universally accepted as the writings of an Essene community living at Qumran on the shores of the Dead Sea – this party has attracted an enormous amount of scholarly attention. This is due in part at least to the very real similarities and parallels with various New Testament writings, but also because the discoveries have given us a whole body of literature from a group within Judaism which documents their beliefs and practices, as well as their self-understanding over against other groups and the way in which they related to the older traditions of Israel. Of course the Essenes cannot be identified simply with the Qumran group, since ancient writers, primarily Josephus and Pliny, had given detailed accounts of the movement since it had attracted quite an amount of attention, and not a little admiration, even in the ancient world. Their decision to withdraw from society and live apart in small communities of caring and sharing is always an attractive ideal for some people at times of special tension in society, and so Essenism could be seen as another illustration of the signs of the times, represented by the Cynics and the Pythagoreans outside Judaism. But it is their place within Judaism that is our chief concern.

When and under what influences did Essenism emerge within Judaism? It is usual to consider their name as derived from the *hasîdîm*, being a graecised version of the Aramaic equivalent, and this connection seems to be confirmed both by what we know from independent sources about the latter and from what the scrolls reveal about the former. During the persecution that went with the implementation of the hellenistic reform we read that many Jews, 'seeking righteousness and justice went down to the desert with their families and their possessions' (fourth citation above), but were followed by the Seleucid officers and as many as one thousand fell by the sword because they refused to fight on the Sabbath. It is probably among such groups as these that we are to see the beginnings of Essenism, since Philo tells us that they fled the cities and lived in villages, considering it impossible to pursue their special life-style otherwise. The Qumran Essenes were founded by a person whom their writings call 'the teacher of righteousness'. Before the teacher's arrival they were a wandering and amorphous group in the wilderness, yet not all Essenes followed the teacher's plea to join him, and subsequently his community saw those who refused as the real religious traitors and their leader is styled 'the man of lies'. Yet another enemy of the teacher is 'the wicked priest', who followed him to the desert and persecuted him, possibly even having him put to death, but the community of his followers kept his memory alive, saw in him the definitive interpreter of God's will for the end of days, and possibly even expected his return.

Naturally there has been much discussion concerning the identity of these various characters since no known historical figure is mentioned in the scrolls or by the ancient writers. One plausible hypothesis is that the wicked priest is Jonathan, the Maccabaean, who accepted the highpriest-hood from the Seleucids in 152 B.C.E., though he was not of the high priestly lineage. The teacher of righteousness would then be identified with a high standing Jerusalem priest, possibly the one who had acted as replacement since the death of Alcimus in 160 B.C.E., and who refused to serve under an illegitimate high priest. These identifications would help to explain certain features of the Qumran community's life and self-understanding, in particular their views about the temple, that central symbol of Jewish faith. According to Josephus the Essenes did not offer sacrifices (though there is some doubt about what precisely Josephus did write), and this seems to be borne out by the scrolls which either speak of the community in its present life as the true temple or alternatively look forward to a temple to come in which the community alone will be able to worship. If then the Qumran community thinks of itself and its own life of prayer, asceticism and study as the true worship of God, this is a clear example of a group appropriating a central symbol of Judaism for themselves alone to the exclusion of all others. Clearly this is both sectarian and highly polemical and the likelihood must be that such attitudes were generated in a situation in which a group and/or an individual were excluded from control of the existing temple. By way of compensation that temple and its priesthood were rejected and an alternative temple-community established, of which those ousted were in total control. This would constitute a good example of the structuring and control of an alternative social world which, we suggested, was typical of an apocalyptically-based community.

The Essenes were certainly highly apocalyptic in their thinking and practice. One of the documents found in the Qumran caves is entitled, 'The War of the Sons of Light against the Sons of Darkness', in which the final struggle between the forces of good, represented by the community and the sons of Belial, or the evil one, is described in great detail. This is a typical motif of all apocalyptic literature, including early Christian (e.g. the final petitions of the 'Our Father'), in which the increase of hostility and evil are thought to be the immediate harbingers of the new age that is about to dawn. One has only to read the so-called 'eschatological discourse' in the Synoptic gospels (Mk 13; Mt 24-25; Lk 21) to appreciate how fully the early Christians shared such ideas and expressed them in similar, if not actually borrowed, imagery.

Corresponding to this view of the times, the Essenes had developed an extremely rigourous code of ethics and life-style as part of the immediate preparation for, if not the ushering in of the messianic age. Again the discovery of the scrolls enables us to document this in great detail especially in the Community Rule, but the broad outlines agree with what the ancient authors (Philo, Josephus and Pliny) had already conveyed. They practised celibacy (though the possibility of some married Essenes cannot be totally ruled out); they shared their goods in common; they lived in a state of ritual purity – a notion to be discussed in detail when dealing with the Pharisees; novices had to go through various stages of initiation before being allowed to partake of the common meals of the sect; members could be expelled, even for life, for various offences; honesty in speech was a particularly cultivated virtue among them. Clearly the asceticism of the Essenes went far beyond that enjoined by Pentateuchal law, or as we shall see even the Pharisaic teachings, and this can be attributed to the sect's apocalyptic mentality. They, and only they, would share in the great triumph soon to be inaugurated by God.

Much has been written about the relations between the Essenes and early Christianity. John the Baptist, and even Jesus himself, it has been suggested, came under Essene influence. Yet despite the natural excitement that such theories are likely to engender, it must be stated that no such direct contacts can be proved, and in truth are unlikely, given the very different viewpoints of Jesus, in particular, and Essenism. The real value of our newly discovered knowledge of this Jewish sect, contemporaneous with the rise of Christianity, is the light it sheds on the pluralism of first century Judaism; for example the way in which such central theological ideas as covenant, repentance and election were understood and the claims that differing groups were likely to make in the name of their own particular ideology. In this respect the study of the ancient texts at Qumran is particularly interesting. The archaeology of their site has been able to locate their *scriptorium* or writing room, and the remains of over 500 volumes have been discovered in the jars, very deliberately hidden in the caves overlooking the settlement shortly before its abandonment, probably in the year 73 C.E. Clearly the sect was devoted to the study and interpretation of the older Jewish writings that were particularly authoritative, even though as yet there does not appear to have been a definitive canon of Scripture, even for this rigid community. Yet side by side with these writings that were the common inheritance of all Judaism, and apparently having equal authority with them, were the sect's own writings, which were also believed to express God's definitive will for the group. Foremost among these is of course the Community Rule, already alluded to. Furthermore, we find some of the prophetic writings being interpreted in relation to events in the community's own life, rather like the way in which several New Testament authors see various Old Testament texts receiving their definitive meaning in the light of Jesus' life and that of the early church (cf. for example Mt 1:23; 2:6; 4:15-17; Lk 4:18-19; Jn 19:36-37; Ac 28:26-27; 2 Cor 3:12-18; Gal 4:21-31). In the final analysis then, the real contribution that the Qumran finds can make to our knowledge of early Christianity is the way they illustrate for us how another Jewish sect contemporaneous with the Jesus movement appropriated the traditions of Israel and blended them with their own special traditions as a way of defining themselves over against all other groups. By understanding the dynamics of this activity we are better able to understand the origins and development of early Christian theology as it engaged in a similar activity, though with a rather different vision, as we shall see.

(iii) THE PHARISEES

Of all the groups within Judaism of the first century, the Pharisees were the most influential, and yet their role and achievement have been largely misunderstood. Part of the reason is that the gospels, especially that of Matthew, are less than kind to them for polemical reasons which we shall discuss later, and the later rabbinic sources tend to blur the distinction between the achievements of the rabbis after 70 C.E. and the Pharisees of an earlier period. Even Josephus, who declares himself to have been a Pharisee, has rather different profiles in his two major works, *The Jewish War* and *Antiquities*. In the former work written shortly after the fall of Jerusalem in 70 C.E. they are not considered to be as significant as the Sadducees, whereas in the latter, written twenty years later, it is the Pharisaic party that is portrayed as the soul of moderation and the real voice of Judaism. Obviously the different objectives of the two works and the change of situation, both for Josephus and Judaism, has affected the picture. We must attempt to reconstruct a more authentic picture of the Pharisees than those which our sources offer and assess their real contribution to Judaism.

Once again it is to the restoration period after the hellenistic reform period that we must look for Pharisaic origins. Essentially the Pharisaic ideal as it emerges in our various sources was that the special ritual purity which applied to the priests in the temple should be extended beyond the sanctuary to the everyday. This suggests that the movement originated among temple priests – presumably because of their dissatisfaction with the existing situation after the restoration, either during Alcimus' tenure of the high-priestly office or after Jonathan's acceptance of it in 152

B.C.E. Unlike the teacher of righteousness, however, their solution was rather to extend the sacredness of the temple to the everyday, thereby minimising the former's significance within the religious life of Judaism but without denying its centrality. Thus, it is better not to think of the Pharisees as a sect in the strict sense, that is a group who excluded all non-Pharisees from the salvation to which they had acquired the indispensable means. The Pharisees never cut themselves off from the temple, and for a period at least they controlled the regulation of temple ritual, according to Josephus. The Essenes, on the other hand, rejected the existing temple worship altogether, and saw membership of their own group as the only alternative means of approaching God and sharing in his promises.

What prompted this movement within the Judaism of the period? The fact that it began with priests, but soon became a lay movement for the most part, suggests that it was intended to meet and in fact did respond to real religious needs within Judaism. Josephus says that the movement was especially successful among townspeople, that is, presumably among the middle class artisans, traders, officials and other service people, whose emergence was the direct result of the economic and social impact of Hellenism, both within Palestine and among the Diaspora. Clearly the founders of Pharisaism were motivated by a zeal for Judaism that was not content with the *laissez-faire* attitudes of the Sadducees after the erosions of Hellenism, and they attempted to build a religious system that went far beyond the demands of the temple religion as this was laid down in the Pentateuch. The annual pilgrimages made for the three great feasts may have been quite adequate expressions of their religion for peasants tied to the land and reminded of Yahweh's continued blessings in the various crops that they were supposed to tithe, but for the Jew who had moved to the new urban environment with no crops to tithe, or at best only token ones (cf. Mt 23:23), Pentateuchal religion was not a sufficient antidote to the spirit of the age. We have seen that already in the Persian period those Jews who had returned from the exile had very definite views on the question of separatism, and Ezra's reform had consolidated their position. We have also traced the background of the *hasîdîm* to these circles. There was nothing more natural then than for those *hasîdîm* who had not adopted the radical views of the Essenes to become enthusiastic supporters of the new movement. The attempted reform had made everybody aware that the threat of Hellenism was much more serious than might have been anticipated because it was so all-pervasive, reaching every area of life, and challenging the Jew to abandon his tradition in the name of 'progress' – economic, social or intellectual.

To meet such a challenge Pharisaism developed a detailed programme of life that preserved his distinctiveness for the Jew no matter where he went or what his walk of life. The detailed legislation for the fulfilment of various central regulations of its system – such as sabbath observance, dietary laws and tithing – went far beyond anything that was found in the Pentateuch. And areas of life not covered at all in the biblical texts were all taken under the umbrella of God's will and legislated for. In time a whole body of Pharisaic teaching developed that was thought of as being of equal authority with the biblical law. It had many different sources: the extension of the biblical law to subjects only indirectly referred to; custom that had developed over a period of time; the teaching of the great sages or fathers. Yet all were regarded as equally binding and expressive of God's will, to such an extent that what the New Testament calls the 'tradition of the elders' and Josephus 'the ancestral laws', were claimed by the later rabbis to be a second, oral law, given together with the written one to Moses on Mount Sinai. Such later statements as these are clearly intended to give full weight and equal authority with the law of Moses to the Pharisaic teachings, but the New Testament is already aware that they were regarded in that light (cf. Mk 7:15; Mt 23:2).

By giving their own customs such an authoritative force the Pharisees have often been accused of turning the Jewish religion into a legalistic system where all the emphasis is placed on externals alone, to the neglect of the interior intention and more important ethical issues. No doubt the Pharisees were no less liable than any other group to fall into these perennial pitfalls of devout-minded people, but to characterise them as lacking in genuine religious concern is to confuse New Testament polemics with historical reality. The Pharisaic system was built on law, conceived however, not as a burdensome obligation, but as instruction or a way of life – the root meaning of the Hebrew word for law, *torah*. There is a real sense in which their achievement can be compared with the Stoic system which, we saw in our first chapter, perceived the whole world as one large city-state governed by the law of nature which assigned to every man his place in society and gave him a definite programme of action for life. The city charter became the cosmic charter, reassuring man that the world was an ordered whole in which each had a definite meaningful role to play. Insofar as Pharisaism was a Jewish attempt to meet the challenge of the city and the hellenistic world-view it can be seen to be giving a similar answer – the *torah* was the very basis and foundation of the universe that each faithful Jew had received as a priceless gift to guide and direct his way, no matter where he lived or what his occupation. Where the Pharisees differed from the Stoics was in their belief that this law as the universal guide of the individual was not based on some abstract reasoning process, but on the gift of Yahweh to his chosen ones. Consequently, the Pharisee did not consider himself to be heavily laden; the yoke of the law was for him a sweet and light burden also.

Precisely because the Pharisaic system was built on law, conceived as statute, that is as having a binding force on man, its masters had to insist on the letter of the law. To admit anything else would be to destroy their system completely. However, no body of statutes, no matter how detailed, can possibly meet every situation, and so there was a real need to develop various ways of dealing with instances not specificaly legislated for, while attempting at the same time to avoid the more harsh (even unjust) consequences of the letter, strictly adhered to. As one example of the kind of problem facing the Pharisaic scribe we may instance a prescription of the sabbatical year which insisted that all debts owed to fellow Israelites be cancelled in that year (Dt 15:3). Clearly such an ideal situation would have less serious social consequences in an agricultural society where barter rather than money was the recognised mode of exchange. However, in the hellenistic age when money was much more frequently employed the Deuteronomic law could have been disastrous. People might use it as a way of avoiding payments of debts, and money would not be so readily available for genuine needs of the poorer people. To deal with this impasse the famous Pharisaic sage Hillel is attributed with having introduced a special legislative measure whereby payment of the debt was guaranteed even after the sabbath year, by means of a legal fiction. According to this arrangement the creditor transferred his debt to a court in a formal document. Since the biblical text said, 'Whatever *of yours* that is with your brother your hand should release', the debt, now considered as being owed to the court, not to a fellow Israelite, was not covered by the sabbath year remission, and so the debtor was liable at any time. One has to appreciate the dilemma of the Jew, convinced that the body of laws he had received was indeed a divine blessing and so to be faithfully adhered to in its every jot and tittle (its minutest letter and even part of a letter), and yet faced with real life situations similar to the one just discussed. Without this appreciation the system can be ridiculed as hairsplitting and even ridiculous. Yet looking to its intention and purpose it is seen as a total way of life that ensures the blessings that the whole *torah*, (i.e. the five books of the Pentateuch with their story of God's saving election of Israel), and not just its legal enactments, had promised.

To live out the Pharisaic ideal was not easy, given the fact that not all Jews, not to speak of the gentile population of Palestine and the Diaspora, were prepared to undertake it. Accordingly, many Pharisees joined together in associations that made it easier for them to live up to their ideal. In the Jewish sources the members of such associations (*haverîm*, as they are called) are contrasted with 'the people of the land', a term, that at least in Jesus' day was not a social description but referred to all those who were suspect of being lax in their observance of the purity and tithing laws which the Pharisees regarded as essential, and so to be avoided. The Pharisaic concern with these laws is attacked in the New Testament (Mk 7:1-20; Mt 23:13-36). Once again, however, before accepting the condemnation at face value it is necessary to understand the meaning of such observances from the Jewish perspective. In the next chapter we shall have occasion to examine some of the reasons for the Christian polemics against them. Both the purity laws (avoiding certain objects that created uncleanness, for example, leprosy, secretions from the sexual organs, dead bodies, certain types of food) and the tithes (paying a certain portion of what one produces to the priests and Levites) are rooted in the Old Testament legal codes. The latter can be understood readily enough: since the land of Israel is Yahweh's gift, a portion of its produce should be given to those who minister at his sanctuary and have no portion in the land for themselves. Naturally economic and social conditions had changed considerably, even to the extent of many Jerusalem priests having become wealthy landowners. In such circumstances, the leasing tenant farmer could scarcely be expected to be meticulous in tithing, yet the Pharisaic system insisted on the letter of 'everything that grows', even to the smallest herb. In this pressing of minutiae we must see a genuine desire to avoid any erosion of the biblical law or its intention. If this led to the undesirable consequences mentioned in Mt 2:23-24 – neglect of the weightier matters – this was clearly a *consequence*, not an *intention* of the Pharisaic ideals. Indeed it is noteworthy that in this passage Jesus condemns this consequence, but does not reject the concentration on the lesser matters as unworthy.

The meaning of the purity laws is more difficult to grasp, especially since from an early stage – even in the Bible itself – purity and impurity are also used as metaphors for moral virtue and vice. There is a danger that we might see this as their only significance and so accuse the Pharisee, as many Christian scholars have done, of failing to draw any distinction between the moral law on the one hand and purely ritual (we might say liturgical rubrics) on the other. The fact that the notions of purity and impurity and rituals for dealing with them are found in many ancient religions and many modern primitive ones, suggests that these concepts do refer to something very real that cannot simply be reduced to a metaphor for something else. This 'real' content, at least as far as the Israelites were concerned, seems to be based on the understanding that there is an order and wholeness about the physical universe, man included, which should not be distorted or changed since these reflect the holiness of God, the Creator. Insofar as certain actions (e.g. irregular sexual behaviour) or animals (e.g. the pig) do not fit into this perceived wholeness of things emanating from the Creator, or appear to stand outside their own recognised class, they are thought of as impure, that is polluting or dangerous. Pollution can be brought on either intentionally or inadvertently, and it can concern matters that are strictly speaking ethical or not, as in the examples cited, but its consequences are the same as far as the society is concerned. A destructive power has been set in motion that must be averted by the performance of certain actions that the community has prescribed, depending on the gravity of the violation. This explains why the purity laws are so detailed since every eventuality must be legislated for to protect the order that is believed to be inherent in the whole of the universe.

To concentrate on the negative aspect of the purity laws would be a mistake, however, since for their faithful observer, they were a constant reminder that God, the Creator of the universal order could be encountered at every turn of life – at meals, in dealing with the animal kingdom, on the way or in the home. The supreme encounter was of course at worship in the temple, and that is why the purity laws of the books of *Leviticus* and *Numbers* are intended for the priests, Levites and others who might enter the sacred precincts. The Pharisees attempted to extend that order to the whole of life, by recognising that the holiness of God was as much part of the *everyday* as it was of the *sacred* day, when people approached the temple in a state of ritual purity. As already mentioned, in order to achieve their goal some Pharisees of stricter observance formed associations which had stringent rules of admission, and whose members could be trusted to have observed all the details of the purity laws as the Pharisaic scribes had elaborated them, especially in regard to the dietary laws. This explains why several of Jesus' disputes with the Pharisees occur in the context of meals (Mk 7:1-2; Lk 7:36; 11:37-40), since he, like many other Jews who did not belong to these associations, did not regard meticulous observance of these rules as an essential part of their religious response. Yet it should be noted that Jesus and the Pharisees did agree on some basic ideas like resurrection from the dead, indicating a common background in the apocalyptic world-view, and we do find him on occasion in their homes (Lk 11:37; 14:1).

This is not to minimise the inevitable clash between the Pharisees and any other Jew who was not prepared to accept their view of what the holiness of God demanded. Moreover, this conviction was expressed in their interest in making converts even from the non-Jewish world (Mt 23:15). The Essenes were also concerned with the notion of purity, but unlike the Pharisees, they had solved the problem by living out their beliefs in isolation from the rest of men by considering that in their community alone the ideal of holiness was realised. The Pharisees on the other hand remained very much within society and in fact played a very influential role in Palestinian politics for over a century, even dominating the legislation of the temple ritual according to Josephus, despite the fact that the Sadducees were the party of the priestly aristocracy. As we shall presently see, it was the Pharisaic ideal as elaborated by their scribes that was to become the official one for all Judaism after the temple was destroyed in 70 C.E. It is from this perspective that one can best appreciate their real significance for the Jewish religion. By extending the holiness of the temple outside and beyond the temple even while it still was the centre of Jewish life, they ensured that the holiness of God would remain a vital reality for Judaism, even when the temple, as its visible symbol, was no more.

(iv) THE ZEALOTS

Even though they are scarcely mentioned in the New Testament, in all probability the Zealots played an important part in Palestinian religious and political life of the first century C.E. Yet the virtual silence of all our sources, except Josephus, makes it difficult to fill in the whole picture, since his own career was too closely involved with what they stood for to be totally objective. He gives two rather different accounts of the origins of the Fourth Philosophy, founded by one Judas the Galilean, in the year 6 C.E. and he never calls them Zealots, a name he reserves for the instigators of the revolt against Rome in 67 C.E. In the *War* account Judas' party is said to have nothing in common with the other Jewish philosophies, whereas in *Antiquities* its members are said to resemble the Pharisees in every respect except in their passion for freedom and their refusal to call any man master but God alone. Though Josephus himself never makes the identification, it is generally, and in my view correctly presumed that the

Fourth Philosophy of Judas is to be identified with the Zealots of the revolt period, and this would explain the two different characterisations of the group within his writings. In the *War* account he is particularly concerned to isolate a small group of lawless individuals as having sole responsibility for the confrontation with Rome despite the fact that he himself was a general of the revolutionary government! As part of this apologetic for the Jewish nation, the most typical name that Josephus employs for Jewish revolutionaries throughout the period is robber, thereby suggesting their unprincipled and selfish motives. The likelihood must be that the links with the Pharisees suggested in the *Antiquities* account are real, and that the Fourth Philosophy (Zealots) does have its roots in the more radical wing of the Pharisaic party. This conclusion will help us to understand their ideology.

When Josephus comes to summing up the situation in Jerusalem during the Roman siege of the years 67-70 C.E. he is able to isolate five different groups, each as bitterly opposed to one another as they were to Rome and the Jewish aristocracy who were seen as collaborationists with Rome. These were: the Zealots, the *Sicarii* (literally, dagger carriers), the Idumaeans, John of Gischala and Simon Bar Giora. Because of this fragmentation some scholars have actually doubted the existence of a unified, revolutionary movement throughout the whole first century, dating from the founding of the Fourth Philosophy by Judas. In this view the existence of the Zealots as a distinct party or sect at the time of Jesus would be seriously called into question. However, this seems an unnecessary conclusion, given the well known character of revolutionary movements to splinter around different personalities just when one might expect a united front against the common enemy on whom all are agreed. In the case of the various groups outlined here it is not difficult to recognise differences between them because of tensions emanating from different social backgrounds – city/country, aristocracy/lower classes and lesser clergy/laity. It is an indication of how deep-seated these tensions were that even though all the groups shared the religious ideology on which the revolutionary party was based, they were still their own worst enemies in the hour of crisis. Josephus paints a sorry picture of the way in which all semblance of religious motivation for the revolt was abandoned, the temple desecrated and the most horrible atrocities committed against fellow revolutionaries or the Jewish aristocracy. Even allowing for a fair amount of exaggeration because of the historian's propagandistic purposes, the whole scenario raises serious questions about the danger of using religion to bolster political or despotic causes.

What was the religious motivation of the Zealots? The passion for liberty and the refusal to accept man as lord except God, attributed by Josephus to the Fourth Philosophy, have a certain archaic ring about them, echoing the earlier Israelite religion. Freedom from slavery was the fundamental Israelite experience of the exodus from Egypt and the second command of the decalogue prohibited the acceptance of any other gods except Yahweh, which the Zealots turned into a political programme for rejecting Roman rule. Rabbinic evidence suggests that a series of stringent religious measures, eighteen in all, attributed to the school of Shammai, were passed in Jerusalem in the period shortly before 70 C.E. It is usual to link these with the takeover of the council by the Zealots after they had insisted on abolishing the loyal sacrifices on behalf of the Emperor in the Jerusalem temple in 66 C.E. In general these measures were directed against any kind of association with gentiles and their attitudes–marriage, food, and images for example. The coins struck by the revolutionaries during the revolt corroborate this, since they are aniconic (i.e. without any image) and bear the inscription 'for the freedom of Zion'. Another element of the Zealot philosophy that was religiously motivated was the use of violent means against the perceived enemies because of the belief that they were engaged in the holy war of the end-time that was to destroy Israel's enemies, an idea expressed in Zachary's hymn on the birth of John the Baptist: 'That freed from our enemies we might serve him in holiness and justice before him all our days' (Lk 1:74-75). This violence on behalf of the kingdom links the Zealot movement with that of the Maccabees a century and a half earlier, who treated Phineas' act of violence on behalf of his Israelite faith as the model for religious resistance (Nm 25:6-14; 1 Macc 2:24-26.54). However, the Maccabees and Zealots differed essentially, it would seem, on the kind of Jewish state they sought. Once political power came their way through the weakness of the Seleucids, the former set up a thoroughly hellenised system in which the monarch controlled the religion also, much to the anger of the religious elements in the community. On the other hand the Zealots would appear to have had in mind the re-establishment of the old theocracy with no concessions to modernity, doing away with the sacrifice for the Emperor and electing by lot an unknown country priest as high priest.

If we accept the existence of the Zealot party as dating from the period of Judas the Galilean, the question naturally arises concerning their relation to the Jesus movement during the same period, especially in view of the fact that at least one member of the Twelve, Simon, the Cananaean, was in fact a Zealot, as Luke explicitly says (Lk 6:15). Besides, such actions as the cleansing of the temple by Jesus and his disciples' desire to use the sword in self-defense (Mk 11:15; Lk 22:49) when taken together with the clear political overtones of Jesus' death, have all been construed as pointing to a strong current of Zealot ideology in Jesus' and his close followers' attitudes. This theory is thought to gain further support from the belief that first century Galilee was a hotbed of anti-Roman revolutionaries, as witnessed by the fact that the founder of the Fourth Philosophy was a native of the province. However, we have argued in the previous chapter that this view is not founded on the evidence, and there is far too much that is central to the preaching of Jesus that is utterly opposed to Zealot beliefs. In particular, sayings about turning the other cheek and loving one's enemies as well as the refusal to be drawn on the question of tribute to Caesar, show that Jesus did not wish to be identified in any way with the Zealots or their views about God's kingdom. This holds true even when popular opinion was anxious to cast him in that role and his enemies who wished to have him removed were able to misrepresent him as a political pretender to the Roman authorities. As we shall see, some of his language could have been construed in purely political terms by those who were looking for such a messianic leader, yet in the end the whole trend of his ministry seems to have been concerned with the religious rather than the political aspects of Judaism. Nor is there any evidence that the Jerusalem Christians were prepared to become embroiled in the national struggle, thus obeying the apocalyptic warnings of certain gospel passages. A later Christian historian, Eusebius, says that they fled to Pella shortly before the outbreak of hostilities, and this would seem to confirm the view that neither Jesus nor his followers who stayed closest to the heart of Judaism ever had any fascination with the Zealot ideal.

IV. After 70 C.E.: The Making of Rabbinic Judaism

In the previous chapter we have seen how the Romans reorganised Palestine in the wake of the destruction of 70 C.E. With the temple destroyed, those groups within Judaism who had taken their religious stance in relation to it were now totally deprived of any basis for their faith, and were consequently forced to rethink their position in regard to the temple and its meaning, or to find another way. We do not know how many of the religious leaders survived the catastrophe. Presumably they were not very many, given the civil strife, as well as the Roman siege and its aftermath. Subsequently we do hear of a group called 'The holy congregation of Jerusalem', who in all probability attempted to retain their identity as Jerusalemites in exile, presumably hoping for the rebuilding of the temple. There is also some evidence of people returning to the temple mount on pilgrimage even after the destruction. Clearly then, the memory of the temple could not be wiped away so easily, something underlined by the fact that the emperor Hadrian's desire to build a temple in honour of the head of the Roman pantheon, Jupiter, in Jerusalem was a major contributory factor to the second Jewish revolt of 132-135 C.E. Yet despite these scattered pieces of evidence, it is clear that the strand of Judaism that was least dependent on visible or political structures for its survival was likely to have been most successful, and it is in this respect that Pharisaism was best equipped to fill the breach.

Later rabbinic sources have a legend about an influential Jerusalem sage of the Pharisaic party, Johanan ben Zakkai, escaping from Jerusalem during the Roman siege in a rather bizarre fashion: he had his disciples carry him out in a coffin, and thus escaped to Vespasian who then allowed him to open a school at the coastal town of Jamnia. It was there that the beginning of the reorganisation was to take place as Johanan, first for his followers, and subsequently for others who joined him, was able to gradually place the study of the Torah rather than the pilgrimage to Jerusalem at the real centre of Jewish life and piety. It is not that this was an unimportant facet of Jewish life prior to 70 C.E. – indeed for centuries. What was different now was that study became *the* centre of Jewish life replacing all others of the previous period. The story is told that on one occasion as Rabbi Johanan was leaving Jerusalem one of his students began to lament at the sight of the temple ruins 'where the sins of Israel were atoned'. But Rabbi Johanan replied, 'I will show you another way', and cited a text from scripture, 'I will have mercy not sacrifice' (Hos 6:6), to indicate that deeds of loving kindness towards the neighbour were as important in God's eyes as were acts of worship. This episode is a good illustration of the direction of Johanan's and his followers' theological position: the destruction of the temple was God's punishment for failure to live out the demands of God's law, and now the study and application of that had to be intensified and extended to all segments of the people. By seeing the calamity in terms of God's corrective judgement Johanan and his successors were able to achieve the double goal of averting a crisis of faith on the one hand and ensuring greater support for his own particular project on the other. The synagogue, whose beginnings we suggested may have been as far back as the Babylonian exile and which had served an important function as a religious as well as a social centre, now takes on increasing importance within Jewish life. Indeed some of Johanan's earliest enactments in his role as quasi-official interpreter of Jewish law, were to transfer certain liturgical practices that had been performed only in the temple to the synagogue. Thus the latter increasingly came to have a sacred character as a 'house of prayer', and many of the prayers and liturgical practices that now make up the Jewish prayer book (the *Siddur*) began to take definite form in this period.

One must not give the impression that Johanan and his successors had an easy passage. There are many traditions of tensions and recriminations between the various Jamnia teachers and their disciples. These are in part due to the different personalities in question, their background in the pre-70 situation and the diverging attitudes of the leading Pharisaic schools (especially those of Hillel and Shammai) from that earlier period. It has often been suggested that what has come to be called 'the Jamnia period' was one of consolidation of Jewish attitudes over against the early Christians, especially the so-called Jewish Christians who had lived in close relation to Judaism up to that time. While there undoubtedly is some truth to the assertion that as a normative version of Judaism emerged clearer lines of demarcation between the two groups were likely to develop, yet a sense of balance is called for. It seems unlikely that there ever was a Council of Jamnia, similar in intent and function to later councils of the Church, which finally pronounced the Christians to be heretics. This is the usual explanation of the *birkath ha-minim*, or blessing (curse) of the heretics which many suggest was introduced into the *Amidah* prayer (also known as The Eighteen Benedictions) at this time. In fact the curse in question is more general in its intent, and in its earliest version is directed against all who are regarded by the emerging orthodoxy as errant, and this presumably included Christians also. We know from the rabbinic sources that at this time there was a real effort on the part of the Jamnia rabbis to extend the obligations of their way to Jews who had fled Palestine, especially to Syria, in the wake of the first revolt. In all probability these refugees included many Christians from Palestine, and this would inevitably have given rise to tensions between groups who had previously been content to live in a loosely defined relationship as various parties in the pluralistic religious environment we described in the previous section. Besides, we hear of bitter dispute between later rabbis and 'the peoples of the land', a term that now applies to all who did not willingly embrace the rabbinic ideal, irrespective of their social background—disputes that continued into the third century C.E. Thus, while the developments within Judaism which we have been describing played a vital role in helping several early Christian groups define their beliefs and structures more precisely — something we shall discuss more fully in our next chapter — the conflicts and mutual recriminations that one finds echoed in the literature (for example, Mt 23), should not be read as though Christians and Jews were already two mutually opposed world religions engaged in deadly polemics against each other. The fall of the temple was a shock to both Jews and Christians, insofar as it pushed people of all religious persuasions in

Palestine (and those in the Diaspora who drew their inspiration from there) to redefine their understanding of their religious convictions, both in terms of the nature and extent of the divine presence and the human response to it. In this regard the fall of the temple was as significant for emerging Christianity as it was for Judaism itself.

Conclusion: Jew and Greek

Our treatment of Judaism of the second temple period has focused almost entirely on Palestine, and our approach has been to show how the historical vicissitudes there shaped the religious response in several different directions. Basically it is an account of Judaism's struggle with the hellenistic world of which it found itself a part since Alexander's conquests. The problem was how to retain the unique sense of election that the Jews had always experienced when the larger cultural situation was pulling in the opposite direction. As we have seen, there are several possible answers to that question ranging from total assimilation to utter rejection, and we have attempted to outline the more important responses. Inevitably our sketch has not captured every facet and in a survey such as this there is a danger of missing the real heart of the matter. In emphasising the varieties and complexities one can easily ignore the spiritual power that came from a firm belief in the God who continued to direct the processes of history, even when these seemed to conflict with the best interests of his chosen people. To grasp this aspect of the Jewish experience it is necessary to recognise that today this same belief is a vital force helping a people to transcend the atrocities of the Nazi concentration camp and celebrate the presence of God in this world discovered in and through his creation. This continuity of vision is ensured through the continuity of prayer life which expresses, better than anything, this people's apprehension of the divine/human encounter. The daily recitation of the *Shema* – 'Hear O Israel, the Lord your God is one Lord' – and the *Amidah* – 'Blessed art thou, Lord our God and God of our Fathers . . .' – are expressions of that faith that span the centuries from the Babylonian captivity and beyond to the present. It is sometimes difficult for Christians who have learned that Christ is the fulfilment of the Jewish hope, to realise that that hope is still alive in the Jewish faith today and finds an authentic expression still in Jewish religious life and worship. Yet this difficulty of the modern Christian has been compounded by scholars who have been all too ready to see the Judaism of the first century as a dried and desiccated root devoid of all genuine religious expression. Hopefully our sketchy treatment will at least succeed in restoring the balance, as a starting point for twentieth century Christians to learn from and with their Jewish brothers from the great treasury that they hold in common, the Hebrew Scriptures.

Our concentration on Judaism as it developed in Palestine should not obscure the developments in the Diaspora, where, we saw, Judaism's encounter with Hellenism was of a different kind to that of the homeland. Yet it was from these communities that Paul and the other Christian missionaries made their first converts, if *Acts of the Apostles* is correct. That these communities had learned to adapt to life in the larger world yet retain their Jewishness is evidenced in their production of the Greek translation of the Old Testament as early as the third century B.C.E. Clearly, within a generation or two of Alexander's death, there were many Jews who no longer spoke the Hebrew tongue, yet felt the need to retain their Jewish faith. It was to meet their needs that the first translation of the Hebrew Scriptures was produced. Other books, expressing the essence of the Jewish faith but in concepts and language drawn from Greek philosophy, were written. Alexandria in Egypt, was one centre of which we know, where this activity was highly developed as the Jewish religious philosopher, Philo (c. 20 B.C.E. – 45 C.E.) amply bears witness. Unfortunately, apart from Philo, hardly any of this literature contemporaneous with Christianity has been preserved for us, and it seems to have made little impact on Palestinian Judaism, at least as this is reflected in rabbinic literature. It is not easy to decide whether Philo is representative of this branch of Judaism, or whether he is merely a voice in the wilderness, attempting to reconcile his intellectual curiosity with his religious faith. The fact that the *Book of Wisdom*, also a product of Alexandria it is thought, shows similar interests, strongly suggests the former. Surprisingly enough, we hear of no great support for either revolt in Palestine from Jews of the Diaspora – though there was a Jewish uprising in Alexandria in 115 C.E. which apparently was Zealot-inspired – and this suggests that at least politically, if not also ideologically, there were real differences between Jews in the homeland and those of the Diaspora. The conflict between the Hebrews and Hellenists in the early church (Ac 6:1) would also seem to support that view. The likelihood must be that Diaspora Jews for the most part had a different outlook on the way in which their Jewishness could be integrated into a hellenistic world-view. This would explain Christianity's appeal for many of them, especially as elaborated by Paul, where distinctive religious ideas based on the Hebrew Scriptures could be integrated with a more positive role for the gentiles in the one universal plan of God. But that suggestion takes us to the final chapter of our study.

4. Christians

4. CHRISTIANS

These twelve Jesus sent out, charging, "Go nowhere among the gentiles, and enter no town of the Samaritans, but go rather to the lost sheep of the house of Israel ... for truly I say to you, you will not have gone through all the cities of Israel before the Son of Man comes" (Mt 10:5-6.23).

For I delivered to you as of first importance what I also received, that Christ died for our sins in accordance with the Scriptures, that he was buried, that he was raised on the third day in accordance with the Scriptures, and that he appeared to Cephas, then to the twelve. Then he appeared to more than five hundred brethren at one time . . . then he appeared to James, then to all the apostles. Last of all, as to one untimely born, he appeared also to me (1 Cor 15:3-8).

And all who believed were together and had all things in common, and they sold their possessions and goods and distributed them to all, as any had need. And day by day attending the temple together and breaking bread in their homes they partook of food with glad and generous hearts (Ac 2:46).

But when Cephas came to Antioch I (Paul) opposed him to his face because he stood condemned. For before certain men came from James he ate with the gentiles; but when they came he drew back and separated himself, fearing the circumcision party. And with him the rest of the Jews acted insincerely, so that even Barnabas was carried away by their insincerity (Gal 2:11-13).

And in Antioch the disciples were for the first time called Christians (Ac 11:26).

For consider your call, brethren; not many of you were wise by worldly standards, not many were powerful, not many were of noble birth (1 Cor 1:26).

Now, brethren, you know that the household of Stephanas were the first converts in Achaia, and they have devoted themselves to the service of the saints (1 Cor 16:15).

In order to dispel the rumour (of his own responsibility for the fire of Rome) Nero shifted the blame to others and imposed the most refined punishments upon people despised for their vices, whom the populace called 'Christians'. The name is derived from Christ; he had been executed by the procurator Pontius Pilate during the reign of Tiberius. For the moment the pernicious superstition was suppressed. But it broke out again, not only in Judaea, the home of the disease, but in the capital itself, where everything atrocious and shameful from everywhere comes together and finds a following (Tacitus *Annals* 15,44).

They (Christians in Bithynia) assured me that the sum total of their guilt or error consisted in the fact that they regularly assembled on a certain day before daybreak. They recited hymns antiphonally *to Christ as (their) God* and bound themselves with an oath not to commit any crime . . . After this it was their custom to separate and then to come together again to partake of a meal, but an ordinary and innocent one (Pliny to Trajan, c. 112 C.E., *Letters* X,96).

IT MIGHT APPEAR superfluous, or even downright arrogant, to attempt to deal in one chapter with the early Christians, seeing that the whole series, of which this is but an introductory volume, is dedicated to the exposition of each of the New Testament books. What is the purpose of compressing into a few pages a topic that appears to call for a much more extensive treatment? This apparently valid criticism loses much of its cogency on a little reflection, however. Our topic – Christians – should not be confused with the New Testament writings or their message, no matter how closely they appear to be related. As is well known the writings that came eventually to be known as the New Testament, and which form part of canonical Scripture for the Christian Church, have a varied compositional history and purpose. No one person or group of persons set out to write the New Testament. Individual Christian teachers, evangelists and missionaries wrote different documents to different Christian communities in the first century, and it is only a selection of that literature that has been preserved for us. Even Paul, who of all the early Christian authors, is by far the best represented in our selection, did not have all his writings survive. We hear for example of a letter to the Laodicaeans (Col 4:16) that is no longer extant, and most scholars believe that Paul's correspondence with the Corinthians was much more extensive than that represented in the two surviving epistles to that Church. In other words, behind the writings which comprise our New Testament, and presupposed by all of them, is the Christian movement with its own chequered history. This is the subject of our present chapter.

To the uninitiated our task might seem to be a rather straightforward one, seeing that one at least of the New Testament writings – *Acts of the Apostles* – purports to trace the history of the Christian movement, taking us from Jerusalem to Rome in a fairly direct line. Yet only a moment's reflection makes one painfully aware that *Acts* raises as many questions as it answers in terms of early Christian history. Mention may be made of just a few of the perplexing obscurities we are left with: what was the fate of Peter and the Twelve who are at the centre of the story up to chapter 6, and then disappear completely, apart from a few brief appearances by Peter? By what circumstances did James, the brother of the Lord, emerge as the leader of the Jerusalem church (cf. Ac 15:13) seeing that the gospels suggest that 'his brothers' did not accept Jesus' claims and were not part of his intimate circle of followers during his lifetime (Mk 3:21.31)? How can we reconcile the account of Paul's relationship to the Jerusalem church with the apostle's own statements in his epistles, especially *Galatians 2*? Why was it only some of the Jerusalem Christians who had to leave the holy city during the persecution connected with Stephen's death (Ac 8:1)? To ask such questions as these must make us aware that the purpose of the author of *Acts* could not have been to give an account of the early Christian movement, even when he appears to be doing just that! He even leaves us with the tantalising presence of Paul in Rome awaiting trial, without telling us the outcome or in what circumstances Paul met his death, something he must surely have known, if, as is commonly held, the author was Luke, Paul's own faithful companion (Col 4:14; 2 Tm 4:11).

Clearly then the task of tracing the development of the early Christian movement is not a simple one. In the absence of information about key individuals and important stages, there must inevitably be some degree of conjecture in any historical reconstruction. Nevertheless, the enterprise cannot be abandoned just because of the problems involved. The very effort even in the absence of absolute certainty, can tell us much that is vital for our understanding of the writings we now possess, which are often written to critique certain developments that have been taking place or to warn against certain trends that are considered erroneous. The early Christian period should not, as is sometimes believed, be considered a golden age from which the movement diverged subsequently. There were tensions and problems from the very start, something that should cause no surprise given the diverse religious picture we have discovered, even within Judaism, originating in the social and cultural pluralism of the times. Christians were no more immune from their world than any other group, and indeed we shall discover that that world played a vital role in determining many of their religious responses and outlooks.

To talk about cultural and social pluralism as a determining factor in the early Christian movement suggests that no single approach will suffice to capture its complexity. Too often the study of our topic has been heavily theological, in the narrow sense of that word. Scholars have approached the early Christian community with certain dogmatic presuppositions related to subsequent church controversies and have inevitably found what they were looking for – confirmation of certain preconceived ideas on one side or another of a later theological dispute. This is not to suggest that theological concerns are not legitimate and important. In the history of a religious movement however, theology may often have to play a subordinate role initially, as other concrete factors touching on the everyday lives of people have a more influential impact on the course of events. Recent studies of early Christianity that have approached the available data with questions posed by such human sciences as sociology and cultural anthropology have given every promise of shedding new light on old questions. Consequently we propose to draw on these insights without neglecting the theological concerns of earlier enquiries. Inevitably not every position adopted in the following outline is beyond dispute, and many may be at variance with those suggested in the various individual commentaries of this series. However, that also can be an instructive experience for the student who is thereby invited to make his or her own judgments about the early Christians and their world, and challenged to discover the truth of those judgements by responding in a Christian fashion to the twentieth century and its world.

I. Jesus and the Early Christian Movement

It might seem that our deliberations up to this point have ignored the most important figure in and for early Christianity, its founder, Jesus of Nazareth. Surpassing all cultural and social differences, belief in Jesus, however differently expressed, gave Christianity its central and unifying force – indeed its very name (cf. fifth and eighth citations). However, we must be careful not to confuse this role for the Christian movement of belief in Jesus as the Christ – a belief that came to be expressed in its full Christian sense only after the resurrection according to Ac 2:36 – with the role of the historical Jesus. In insisting on this distinction between the contribution of Jesus during his lifetime and that of belief in Jesus after his death, we have no wish to make our own the common liberal position which states that Jesus preached the kingdom and the church emerged. The usual intention of a statement such as this is to suggest that there was no continuity between Jesus and the church that came into being after his death. Such a radical discontinuity has been proposed on both theological and historical grounds relating to the purpose and nature of the gospels that cannot be discussed here. It will be sufficient to state that in attempting to separate Jesus' historical activity in relation to the movement that was later to emerge around his name from the impetus that belief in that name gave to the movement at a later stage, we are merely calling for an historical perspective that the New Testament writings themselves bear witness to on every page.

It is inconceivable that the later Christian movement based on belief in Jesus' name could have been thought of let alone succeed, were it not for the fact that there was an actual historical contribution from those who were followers of Jesus during his lifetime. Yet to make such an obvious yet vitally important claim should not be interpreted as though Jesus had planned in advance for every subsequent eventuality or given a fully developed ecclesiastical charter for his followers to implement after his death. To claim this latter position is to ignore the contribution of Paul, as well as others who had never known Jesus. The foundational role of Jesus in regard to Christianity can and should be stated in a way that avoids the kind of historical myopia – to take a current example – that claims that because Jesus chose (and ordained as priests – so the argument goes) twelve *men*, women are permanently excluded from orders by divine law. The later church clearly attached a theological significance to the twelve by calling them apostles – a development most marked in Luke's writings – since this was a current term to which Paul at an early date had given theological depth in relation to his own call. However the probabilities are that Jesus in choosing twelve had in mind the ancient patriarchal structure of God's people based on the twelve tribes (cf. Mt 19:28; Lk 22:28-30), and that in doing so he wished to make claims for his own community as the true Israel. The fact that the church felt no need to institutionalise the office of the twelve as a permanent feature of its life is a sure sign that it recognised the real symbolism of Jesus' choice, and found other appropriate ways of expressing his meaning without following the letter of the ordinance. To suggest that Jesus in choosing males intended to exclude women from ordination, especially in view of the clan idea that stands behind the patriarchal system, is ultimately to do a disservice to his true foundational role in regard to the later Christian movement. It insists on the non-essentials and distracts from what is basic, namely his understanding of the divine promises to mankind as these were expressed in the Judaism of his own day.

What then is the historical Jesus' contribution to the later Christian movement? There is general agreement, even among scholars sceptical of the historical reliability of the gospels, that the dominant idea of Jesus' life and ministry was the notion of the kingdom of God as this was current in Jewish apocalyptic. Central to that conception, we saw, was the doctrine of the two ages, whereby the pious ones looked to a new age in which they would be rewarded for their perseverance and share in the blessings that God was about to inaugurate for his faithful ones. Jesus shares this vision of the divine plan, but with a very important qualification. Whereas others expected the kingly rule of God to erupt with a blinding definiteness that would destroy the wicked and vindicate the just, Jesus proclaimed the kingdom as already present in his own life and ministry. In his view it was characterised not by judgment but by God's mercy and love for all – and especially for those who might be thought of as unworthy according to the ideals of the *hasîdîm* and their heirs within the various parties. Ultimately then, the real difference between Jesus and the other contemporary religious spokesmen within Judaism results from their differing conceptions of where, when and under what conditions the divine presence that is the God of the Fathers was to be encountered. Differences on this fundamental issue inevitably manifested themselves in other areas like community structures, the place of ritual and the moral response that was expected and appropriate, as the community that developed around Jesus' vision began to emerge and define itself. It was only at that later stage that it became possible to speak of Christians as distinct from Jews, and we shall pursue that development presently. First, however, it is necessary to focus more sharply on the distinctiveness of Jesus' vision for his own contemporaries within Judaism, for herein lies the foundational role of the historical Jesus for the early Christian movement.

It has often been claimed that what really differentiated Jesus' point of view was the shift in the temporal perspective – for him God's kingly rule was no longer future but present.

This presence may indeed be hidden and obscured like the treasure that lies buried (Mt 13:44) or the seed that grows mysteriously (Mk 4:26-29), but its hiddenness makes it no less real for those who are in search of treasures or, alternatively, waiting for the harvest. Modern studies of the parables stress the new and creative way that Jesus used this traditional teaching genre to awaken, surprise, even shock his hearers into an awareness of the reality that was in their midst without the apocalyptic fanfare of popular expectation. While all this is undoubtedly true it would scarcely have marked Jesus as the radical religious revolutionary he was considered to have been. According to Ac 5:33-39 such an influential Pharisaic scribe as Gamaliel I, Paul's teacher, was prepared to let the new movement take its course and attempt to authenticate its claims that it was from God. At Qumran the teacher of righteousness and his followers clearly experienced the presence of the new age in their own community which they can describe as 'the covenant which God established with Israel forever in the land of Damascus'. Throughout the whole first century a series of Zealot leaders presented themselves as messianic figures who were about to launch the final holy war against evil, now embodied in Roman power and oppression, and apparently both Jesus (Jn 6:15) and Paul (Ac 21:38) could easily have been regarded in a similar light. In itself then, there was nothing startlingly new in the proclamation of God's kingly rule, even in its final phase, as present and operative. Besides, even in Jesus' view the presence of the kingdom now was merely a sign of the consummation of the age when the apocalyptic hope would soon be realised in all its finality. As the first citation at the beginning of this chapter suggests, there was an urgency about the present in view of that coming consummation, and so in this regard Jesus did not break completely from the apocalyptic expectations of his contemporaries.

The focus suggested earlier that would concentrate on Jesus' view of how and where the divine presence might be experienced is perhaps more helpful than that which seeks to isolate the temporal aspects alone. As we have seen, for all of Judaism the temple was the focal point of that presence and the various groups defined themselves in relation to it – Sadducees controlling it, Pharisees extending its sphere of influence to the everyday, Essenes substituting the desert community for it, Zealots extending it geographically and politically to control of the land. Jesus too seems to have defined himself in relation to it by suggesting that the reality which the temple symbolised, namely the divine presence (cf. Mt 23:16-22), was available and accessible independently of the temple building and its ritual in his own person and life. This seems to be the basis for the charge against him, reported in all the accounts of the trial, that he would destroy the temple and build another (cf. Mk 14:58). The charge is rightly called false in the sense that Jesus clearly did not mean his claims of building another temple to be taken literally, and in fact be seems to have shown great respect for the existing temple, its festivals and ritual. Nevertheless, the fact that the question should arise at all in the context of official reaction to Jesus is a sure sign that there lay the real issue between him and the various other groups within Judaism.

By claiming that the divine presence, defined both as God's kingly rule and as Father, was accessible to people in his own life and person, Jesus undercut the various systems that had been devised within Judaism to control that presence and people's access to it. Therein lay the source of power within actual Palestinian life for parties like the Pharisees and Sadducees, and the aspirations to power of other groups like the Essenes and Zealots. Insofar as Jesus' claims suggested alternative means of access to God, or better, of God's coming to people, outside and independently of all of the groups and their programmes, and to the extent that this had been found attractive, he was clearly striking at the very reasons for existence of each of the groups and their philosophies. To do so in the name of God's final and irrevocable promises to his people was intolerable. At an earlier period the Essenes and their founder had made radical claims of a similar nature and they too had drawn on themselves the ire of those in charge of the temple, in the person of 'the wicked priest' of the Qumran documents. What had eventually made the Essenes tolerable was the fact that they had withdrawn and isolated themselves from all but the few rigorists who were prepared to undergo their ascetical practices. Jesus' wandering charismatic ministry in their midst, and his wide appeal, at least initially with the country people, made him a much more serious threat to the religious establishment, Pharisaic scribes and Sadducean priestly authorities alike.

We know from Jewish sources that the famous Jerusalem sage Johanan ben Zakkai, who was to become the key figure in the reorganisation of Judaism at Jamnia, had been singularly unsuccessful in his attempts to extend scribal influences to Galilee in the pre-70 C.E. period. Given his wide popularity, Jesus' apparently cavalier attitude towards the niceties of scribal regulations was a major obstacle in their attempts to extend the Pharisaic way to all the people. It is not at all surprising then to find that the gospels have preserved a memory of the scribes *from Jerusalem* disputing with him in Galilee (Mk 3:22; 7:1). On the other hand the high priests see the thrust of Jesus in relation to their own centre of power, the temple, and their right, recognised by the Romans, to be in charge of it. Should the Jesus movement suggest an alternative religious way within Judaism, Roman provincial administration could not be expected to make subtle distinctions in regard to a religion that they did not understand and for which they had little sympathy. Against this background the statement attributed by the author of the Fourth Gospel to the chief priests and the Pharisees meeting in council – 'if we let him go on thus, everyone will believe in him, and the Romans will come and destroy both our holy place and our nation' (Jn 11:47-48) – has all the ring of probability about it. Because they shared the role of outsider with him, the Zealots apparently considered that they had found in Jesus the kind of charismatic leader who embodied their own ideals (cf. Jn 6:14-15).

However, once it had become apparent that his understanding of God's kingly rule could embrace both Zealot loyalist (Simon, the Zealot) and Roman collaborationist (Levi, the tax collector) within the same intimate group of followers, they showed little further interest in him (cf. Mk 12:13-17).

In the foregoing discussion of Jesus' relations to the differing Jewish groups of his own day, it has not been our intention to suggest that those other groups either espoused a debased form of religion or were hypocritical – opinions that are all too easy for Christians to espouse, given the rhetoric of the centuries. Nor can we subscribe to the idea that Judaism, or more accurately, Pharisaism made people proud, self-centred and lacking in due reverence for God's saving actions on their behalf. One has only to read Jewish prayers to realise how deeply conscious all Jews were and are of the holiness of God and of his partnership with his people in sanctifying the creation. It should be remembered that Jesus shared certain very fundamental ideas with some of the groups, despite the atmosphere of conflict that surrounds their encounters. With the Pharisees, he believed in the resurrection and the presence of God outside the temple, and he also shared in their rejection of the political aspirations of the Zealots; he joined with the Essenes in their intense experience of the kingdom of God as present, yet he refused to share in their critique of the existing temple and its priesthood or their limitation of that presence to the perfect. Above all, of course, Jesus shared with all groups the belief in the one God of the *Shema* (cf. Mk 10:18) who is the God of Abraham, Isaac and Jacob (cf. Mk 12:26-27). However, Jesus knew this God in a way that was not perceived by the others and it was this insight that he shared with his followers and for this understanding he lived and died. God's initiative in coming to man was not through the instruments of *torah* or temple, but personally and without regard to man's previous spiritual condition. Consequently, while these signs were still sacred in Jesus' view, they no longer held absolute authority as the sole symbols of the divine presence to Israel. Instead they must be understood in the light of this new and final manifestation and interpreted accordingly. Those who previously had charge of *torah* and temple no longer had control of the way in which these were to be used and understood for Jesus and his followers. While there is little enough evidence that Jesus was ever engaged in any extended activity among non-Jews, his understanding of God's rule inevitably pointed in that direction, and as we shall see, the Jesus movement would finally be more at home in Diaspora Judaism and its active missionising, than in its Palestinian matrix. Yet this development only took place in the wake of events which we will presently discuss and this underlines the fact that both Jesus and his movement saw themselves not as inaugurating a new religion, but as the final and definitive voice of the old.

By describing in terms of 'resurrection from the dead' their conviction that God had vindicated Jesus and his claims, his first followers remained within the framework of Jewish apocalyptic hope, where this idea had first been articulated. There is no need here to enter into a discussion of the nature of the resurrection experience or to debate the reliability of the evidence that leads the first followers to proclaim that Jesus was raised by God. It is quite sufficient for our purposes to realise that in one of the earliest pieces of evidence that we have about the meaning of this conviction for their lives (1 Cor 15:3-8, second citation above), they claimed that the Risen Lord authenticated certain figures and groups attached to them who were subsequently to play a vital role in the history of the early church. In other words the resurrection, understood as the vindication of Jesus' claims about the God of the Fathers *and* as the authorisation of the first community leaders, becomes the bridge between the founding role for Christianity of the historical Jesus and his role as the object of Christian faith and worship. The three leaders that are mentioned are Peter, the leader of the Twelve, James and all the apostles, and Paul, like one ultimately born, but destined to have an enormous impact on the development of Christianity. In the subsequent sections of this chapter we propose to address the questions of who the Christians were by following the historical and geographical approach suggested by these three individuals and their spheres of influence; secondly we shall seek to answer our question from the point of view of the sociological and anthropological insights already alluded to. Finally we shall discuss the question from the point of view of the differing theological perspectives that can be detected within our sources.

II. Who Were The Christians?
Historical and Geographical Approaches.

Some historians have questioned Luke's picture which makes Jerusalem the place where the first believers encountered their Risen Lord and prefer instead the tradition that claims that the first appearance took place in Galilee. The point is to some degree irrelevant in that it is only about the community in Jerusalem that we have any information and it is there that we must begin our survey. We get a very idealised picture of the first group, as out third citation suggests. Like the Essenes of Qumran they share everything in common and so there is no needy brother. Their special liturgical life was based on the home and yet, consistent with Jesus' own attitudes, there was no break with the temple and its liturgy. The idyllic nature of this existence taken in conjunction with the fact that it is a summary written purposely by Luke to help the flow of his narrative and lacking any 'hard' facts does raise questions about its reliability. Yet there is no denying that given the apocalyptic thinking of Jesus and his first followers which inculcated a total disregard for this world's goods (Mt 10:9-11; 19:16-22; Mk 6:8-10), there is nothing inherently improbable about the picture.

Accurate or not, this situation was soon to be disrupted by differences that can only be described as social and cultural as well as religious. Much has been written about the Hebrews and the Hellenists who suddenly appear in Ac 6, and this much at least seems certain – insofar as they represent two different language groups within the earliest body of believers they clearly indicate that two very different currents of ideas are to be found within Christianity from the start. As Luke presents the story of the election of the seven deacons to ensure that the Greek widows receive a fair share of the daily distribution of goods, the affair appears innocent enough. Yet the sequel reports that Stephen, one of the seven, suddenly emerged as the spokesman for a severe critique of 'the holy place and the law' and claiming that Jesus would destroy the temple and change the customs which Moses had given (Ac 6:13-14). Stephen (and presumably all the other deacons – all with Greek names) are not just dispensers of community goods but independent Christian preachers and missionaries, side by side with Peter and the Twelve and not obviously subordinate to them, though they could have originally belonged to the 'five hundred brethren' or 'all the apostles' of 1 Cor 15:6f. In all probability they represent a Greek-speaking community of believers that had been established (presumably because of language difficulties in the liturgical celebrations) on lines similar to different Jewish synagogues in the one city for people of different ethnic or language backgrounds (cf. Ac 2:8-11; 6:9). In fact Stephen's real opponents seem to come precisely from such synagogues, representing Jews who had returned to Jerusalem out of zeal for their religion. To find that one who possibly had the same background as themselves was now attacking such sacred institutions as the temple and the *torah* of Moses in the name of Jesus was more than they could accept, and in all probability it was they who instigated his death, not after due process, but rather as an act of 'lynch law'.

This incident of Stephen and the Hellenists is particularly illuminating not just because it introduces us to some of the theological ideas current within the earliest group of believers, but also because it shows that not all branches of the Jesus movement were seen in the same light by the Jewish religious authorities. After Stephen's death we hear of a persecution that forced many within the new movement to leave Jerusalem, with the notable exception of the apostles. Later we find a Christian community in the holy city without any suggestion of a return (Ac 9:26, for example), and so evidently it was only those who belonged to the Hellenists and their sympathisers who were under attack. In fact they became the first missionaries spreading the word about Jesus through the cities and towns of Palestine, especially it would seem in those places where there was a strong Greek influence – Samaria, Caesarea, Tyre, Sidon, Gaza.

It is noteworthy that this first missionary activity originated not with the first followers of Jesus (Peter and the Twelve) but rather among Greek-speaking Jews from various Diaspora situations who had come to see in Jesus the fulfilment of those religious aspirations that had brought them back to Jerusalem in the first place. In that fulfilment not just Jews but Gentiles also were seen to be included in the plan of God, and it was this universal outlook, fostered no doubt by their hellenistic background and experience that enabled them to see the full implications of the new faith in Jesus and the real significance of his openess to all, as this was remembered in the stories about him and his sayings that they had received. Nor should it surprise us that their most bitter opponents were, like themselves, Diaspora Jews whose religious quest had also taken them back to Jerusalem, but who did not share the convictions of their fellow Hellenists about Jesus. One of the persecutors, Saul, was himself to experience similar treatment when he too 'discovered Jesus' and displayed a similar openness to the gentiles. He was treated with suspicion by the followers of Jesus who had stayed on in Jerusalem, presumably because they did not feel easy with his recently discovered liberal attitudes in regard to his former beliefs (Ac 9:26-30), and their reserve was matched by the hostility of fellow Jews from Asia Minor who accused him of profaning the temple by bringing a gentile into the sacred precincts – a crime punishable with death (Ac 21:21.28).

While the Hellenists were engaged in the spreading of the message about Jesus, developments were also taking place in Jerusalem. Perhaps the most remarkable event was the emergence of James, the brother of the Lord, as the leader of the Christians there, given the fact that the gospels suggest the hostility of 'the brothers of the Lord' to Jesus during his life (Mk 3:31; Jn 7:1-6). Apparently, it was a resurrection experience that convinced James at last about the truth of Jesus' claims (cf. second citation above), but the circumstances of his emergence as head of the Jerusalem church can only be surmised. Peter (and presumably the rest of the Twelve) were able to remain in Jerusalem after Stephen's death and the persecution of the Hellenists (Ac 8:1.14). Subsequently, however, they must have only been in infrequent contact with the new movement in the city, for we find Peter at Joppa (Ac 9:43) and later at Antioch (Gal 2:11; but cf. Gal 1:18; 2:9; Ac 11:1; 15:7), and 1 Cor 9:6 tells us that he engaged in missionary activity, taking his wife with him. In all probability the martyrdom of James, the son of Zebedee and one of the original Twelve, by Herod Agrippa I was the turning point in terms of the Jerusalem church and its leadership (Ac 12:2,17). It must have been evident, even at that early stage that official Judaism would not tolerate this growing movement at its centre, at least insofar as its leaders were continuing the critique of Jesus. Apparently James, the Lord's brother, was acceptable in a way that others of the original followers were not. Indeed his earlier opposition to Jesus might have been in his favour now. Besides, later legends about James the Just, as he is called, insist on his devotion to the temple and his deep commitment to Jewish piety. It is in his role as leader of a church that presumably shared his loyalties that he speaks at the council in Jerusalem, representing a decidedly Jewish attitude towards the question of gentile Christians on the basis of Lev 17-18 and in accordance with current practice among Diaspora Jews: 'My judgement is that we should not trouble those of the gentiles who turn to God, but should write to them to abstain from pollutions of idols and from unchastity and from what is strangled and from blood' (Ac 15:19-20; cf. also Ac 21:20-22).

Despite the fact that James and his followers were able to continue in Jerusalem when other leaders of the Christian movement were either persecuted (Peter and John) or executed (Stephen and James the son of Zebedee), he too eventually incurred the ire of the Jewish religious leaders. Josephus tells us that in 62 C.E. before the new procurator Albinus was able to assume office, Ananus the high priest and son of the Annas who had been party to the condemnation of Jesus (Jn 18:12-24), had James and some of his followers condemned to death by stoning, most probably on religious grounds. It is difficult to isolate the motives for this sudden outburst, but whatever they may have been it seems certain that it brought an end to the Christian community in Jerusalem, at least for some time. Eusebius, the later church historian, says that shortly before the outbreak of the first revolt the Christian community migrated to the Roman town of Pella in the Decapolis on the basis of a vision, and this occurrence seems to have an echo in the gospels also (cf. Mk 13:14-22). While Eusebius links the destruction of the city with the death of James for apologetic reasons, it does not seem improbable that the Jewish Christians would flee the city in the wake of Ananus' purge, that is in 62 rather than 66 C.E. Certainly we do hear of Christians in the region of Pella much later, mainly heterodox groups such as the Ebionites and the Nazoraeans, claiming Jesus as their founder, and still holding on to various Jewish practices. Some of them must have returned to Jerusalem at a later time for we also hear from Eusebius of other descendants of the Lord as leaders of the Christian community there. However, neither those who returned, nor those who stayed in the Transjordan region were to play any significant role in the life of the later church, which was to develop more and more independently of its base on Jewish soil.

One non-Palestinian centre that seems to have played a very significant role in this development was Antioch, the capital of the Seleucid kingdom and a thoroughly hellenised city, even though Jews had lived there from its foundation, c. 300 B.C.E., and enjoyed the civic rights of which we spoke earlier. According to our fifth citation above it was in Antioch that the followers of Jesus were first called Christians, presumably because it was there that their distinctive character as a new religion – and not just a Jewish sect – clearly emerged for the first time. What were the reasons for this separation and what problems did it give rise to? In all probability the missionising Hellenists eventually reached Antioch also, since one of Stephen's group was Nicolaus, a proselyte of Antioch, and the account in *Acts* tells us that some of those who had been dispersed from Jerusalem, men of Cyprus and Cyrene, proclaimed the gospel to the Greeks of Antioch (Ac 11:19). Apparently the instigator of this move was Barnabas, subsequently a companion of Paul on his first missionary journey (Ac 13:2), himself a native of Cyprus and a devout Jew before his conversion (Ac 4:36). Barnabas has been overshadowed by the towering figure of Paul the apostle, yet it was he who introduced the latter to the church at Antioch, bringing him from Tarsus, where, apparently, Paul had gone after his conversion (Ac 11:25; cf. 9:30). The author of *Acts* subsequently suggests that the two men separated because of a personal difference (Ac 15:37-39), but in all probability the rift went deeper than that. Initially Paul and Barnabas were openly engaged in preaching to gentiles at Antioch and apparently continued in this vein on their missionary travels through Cyprus and Asia Minor, arousing hostility from the Jews of the Diaspora as they went, presumably because of their unrestricted acceptance of gentiles into the church. It was this issue that gave rise to a serious dispute in the Antiochene church also, eventually calling for a decision from the Jerusalem-based authorities (Gal 2:1-10; Ac 15:1-29). It would appear that it was on the occasion of the implementation of this decision that the two men separated since Paul himself, in his version of the affair in the Epistle to the Galatians (fourth citation above), says that even Barnabas, as well as Peter and others, was hesitant about eating with gentiles when they were under surveillance by certain members of the Jerusalem church, thus violating Paul's understanding of the compromise that had been reached.

The issue was clearly a very sensitive one in the early church, since it called for a whole new understanding of the movement's relations with Judaism, thereby explaining the new name that emerged at Antioch. We shall discuss its theological implications in more detail presently, as here we are chiefly concerned with the way in which it determined the nature and development of the mission. It is significant in this regard to note that Paul's subsequent association with Antioch was very tenuous (Ac 18:22), because, it would appear, the church there, or at least the community to which Paul was attached, was a 'bridge' church which attempted to play a mediating role between Paul's aggressive missionising of gentiles and the Jerusalem community's rather conservative attitudes on the matter. In this regard Peter and Barnabas were more comfortable with this middle position that had been formulated in relation to current Jewish practice, and presumably it was their view rather than that of Paul that prevailed at Antioch. Many scholars believe that the Gospel of Matthew was written at Antioch much later, after the fall of Jerusalem, and they have often been perplexed by various apparently conflicting attitudes that are at once very conservative in regard to Jewish matters (e.g. Mt 5:17-21; 23:2) and yet highly critical of alleged attitudes within Judaism (e.g. Mt 6:1-19; 21:43; 23:13-36; 27:24-26). These views would be very much at home in the situation we have been describing and which Peter and Barnabas were attempting to contain. It was an atmosphere that was likely to have continued, even intensified, after 70 C.E. with the influx of large numbers of refugees, Jewish and Christian, from Palestine. It would also explain the particularly prominent position of Peter as head of the community, reflected in this same gospel (cf. Mt 16:16-19).

At this point we must attempt to assess Paul's role in the new movement, conscious that this calls for a much more detailed discussion than is possible here. One major problem is the reconciling of the picture Paul himself presents in his letters with that of *Acts*. In the former, Paul, at least in the view of many commentators, is an independent apostle, conscious of his mission from the Risen Christ, and the sole authority in the churches which he founded, while according to *Acts* he is subservient to the Jerusalem apostles, a churchman whose career is marked by subservience to a church organisation existing before him. There is no denying that the two portraits do have rather different emphases, but this should not obscure the fact that there is essential agreement on Paul's contribution to the new movement in his deliberately chosen role as apostle of the gentiles. Even when a full reconciliation of the two accounts does not seem possible, as for example in the case of the Jerusalem Council's decree, already mentioned more than once, it is quite possible that we are hearing two different sides of the same debate. Paul highlights his authorisation to accept the gentiles without demanding that they become Jews, and Luke's version agrees, but adds a rider about gentiles respecting Jewish atittudes in certain areas. It was this rider and its interpretation that was to cause the problems for Paul as his converts increasingly came from gentiles who had little or no contact with the synagogues of the Diaspora, either as proselytes or God-fearers. Discrepancies of fact between the two accounts remain, as for example the question of Paul's journeys to Jerusalem (*Acts* has three and *Galatians* two), yet the fundamental fact remains that Paul never once understood himself to be setting up a church independent of the movement that existed before him, however much he may have stressed his own authority and/or independence on occasion (cf. for example 1 Cor 9:1-2; Gal 2:6; 2 Cor 10:7-10). He recognised the presence of other missionaries in the field (1 Cor 1:12; 3:4-5), especially Peter (Gal 2:7); he does not encroach on another's territory (Rm 15:20), yet he has a great desire to share spiritual (Rm 1:11) as well as material (Rm 15:25; 2 Cor 8:4) goods with different churches he has not founded. Perhaps nothing illustrates better the real ties that existed between Paul's churches and others (in this case the Jerusalem one), than the collections for the poor, which became a major preoccupation with him, despite his theological differences with the Jerusalem-based Christians (cf. 1 Cor 16:1; Gal 2:10; 2 Cor 8-9; Rm 15:24-27). Here was a practical sign of unity and brotherhood surpassing all differences of theology and culture.

In attempting to assess Paul's contribution to the new movement it is important to recognise his own background, something he himself stresses more than once. There can be no doubting his devotion to Pharisaic Judaism before his conversion, even though some have queried his claims to have studied with the influential scribe Gamaliel (Ac 22:3; 26:4), because his writings reflect the attitudes of a hellenistic Jewish education rather than those of a Palestinian one. However, this need not be decisive. As a Jew born in the Diaspora the very fact of his presence in Jerusalem is indicative of his intense loyalty to the ancestral religion despite having been brought up in the cosmopolitan environment of Tarsus, 'no mean city', as Paul rather proudly remarks. Clearly, this double background was of enormous significance for his future ministry, starting with his mastery of two (probably three) languages – Greek, Aramaic and

Hebrew. This must have played a part in his ability to relate to people of non-Jewish background subsequently, being Greek to the Greeks and Jew to the Jews that he might win some (cf. 1 Cor 9:19-23). Furthermore Paul was an urban man, with his own trade as tentmaker, which should not be taken to suggest that he was necessarily from an inferior social class. We saw in the last chapter that his Roman citizenship is taken for granted in *Acts*, and especially in the East this presupposes a relatively high social level. Yet too much should not be made of Paul's hellenistic background. By comparison with Philo of Alexandria for example, his familiarity with Greek philosophical trends is second hand, even though passages like Rm 2-3 and the various lists of vices and virtues scattered throughout his letters reflect commonplace hellenistic moral instruction and exhortation. Besides, the style of his letters and the way in which he develops his argumentation also reflect contemporary rhetorical devices. Indeed some scholars have pointed out that Paul would have been perceived as a sophist by his pagan contemporaries, that is, as a philosophic orator and moralist rather than as a religious teacher, seeing that his letters reflect relatively little interest in Christian ritual and are far more concerned with knowledge and conviction, especially as these are reflected in the moral life.

There is no need to rehearse here the details of Paul's missionary journeys which brought him from Asia into Europe as he visited the major cities of the eastern Mediterranean, making Corinth and Ephesus two of his longest stops, but spending some time at Philippi, Thessalonica and Berea also. One piece of detailed information in Ac 18:6 helps us to date Paul's career, for we read that he was taken before the proconsul Gallio in Corinth. An inscription discovered at Delphi referring to this proconsulship dates its beginning to the eleventh (or possibly twelfth) year of the Emperor Claudius' rule, that is 51/52 C.E. The council of Jerusalem is dated two or three years earlier in 49 C.E.

by most scholars, but beyond that it is difficult to be specific about the chronology of any of the events of Paul's life.

We are particularly in the dark about the end of Paul's life, though tradition dating from as early as the end of the first century C.E. claims that he was martyred in Rome, together with Peter. The persecution of Christians under Nero is generally accepted as the only obvious occasion for this occurrence, but unfortunately *Acts* leaves us in the dark about the immediate circumstances. It concludes with Paul in Rome under some form of restrictive detention but able to conduct a ministry of evangelisation, about the years 60-62 C.E. (Ac 28:16). Whether or not he was ever able to visit Spain as he had proposed (Rm 15:24) must remain a matter of conjecture since we have no reliable information on the matter, though needless to say, there has been plenty of speculation based on later legends.

Paul's missionary plan was to establish a community and after a certain period of time to move on to another centre. *Acts* indicates that Paul went first to the Jewish synagogues and only turned to the gentiles after being rejected by the Jews, and the author suggests that this is in accordance with the divine plan of salvation – Jew first and then the gentile. There is nothing improbable about this tactic given the fact that the Diaspora synagogues were centres where not only Jews but gentiles who were attracted to Judaism congregated, and it would be natural for Paul as well as other travelling preachers to visit them. The author of *Acts,* writing at a time when the church and the synagogue were two well defined and opposing entities, suggests that Paul had little success among the Jews and so one gets the impression of a certain stereotyped pattern, yet it seems to be corroborated in a general way in Paul's letters and the controversies generated in the various churches. In fact the question of who precisely Paul's opponents were in the various churches has given rise to a lively debate among scholars, but it is an important key to understanding the drift of his argument and the various emphases in the different letters. The general tendency is to distinguish two essentially different sets of opponents usually designated as the Judaisers, that is, those who attacked Paul's acceptance of gentiles into the new movement without insisting on some degree of observance of Jewish practices (especially in *Galatians* and *Philippians*), and the Gnostics, that is those who espoused some form of elitism within the movement and whose philosophical views about matter and the universe led to a number of unacceptable positions in regard to sexuality, resurrection and the person of Christ (Corinthian correspondence and *Colossians*). The two different trends are not necessarily mutually exclusive, depending on whether or not Paul's opponents are thought to be Jewish or Jewish Christian, and the extent to which it is believed that gnostic ideas had affected various Jewish groups already in the first century.

These controversies help us to understand Paul's relations with his communities, especially the Corinthian correspondence. He receives bulletins from certain groups within the community (cf. 'Chloe's people' 1 Cor 1:11), they exchange letters several times (1 Cor 5:9; 7:1; 2 Cor 2:4) and he sends such messengers as Timothy and Titus (1 Cor 4:17; 2 Cor 7:6) and finally he himself visits them. Clearly it is an intimate and enduring bond that is not at all terminated with Paul's departure elsewhere, or even his imprisonment (cf. 2 Cor 11:23). Little wonder then that even after his death Paul continued to exercise great influence. As was common in the ancient world, letters were written in his name, probably by intimate followers, authorising certain attitudes and positions that were deemed necessary. Even during his life there is evidence that his letters were exchanged by various churches (Col 4:16) and naturally this development was accentuated after his death, so that the corpus of Pauline letters was probably the first part of the New Testament canon to be established.

We must constantly bear in mind that early Christianity defined itself in relation to Judaism, indeed understood itself as a movement within Judaism, if we are to appreciate the impact that the fall of Jerusalem and its temple had on all branches of the new movement. In the previous chapter we saw how, in the wake of the catastrophe, Judiasm as a whole discovered 'the other way' of *torah* to replace the temple's central significance. In all probability this event pushed various Christian groups to redefine their own identity in a way that they were not previously called to do. For those Christians who had remained close to the temple and its worship until the jealousy of the high priest had destroyed their leader, James, it was seen as God's way of vindicating their claims about Messiah Jesus and his judgement on their fellow Jews who had persecuted them. For others, like the Hellenists and the gentile Pauline churches, it was a confirmation of the apostle's gospel of liberty. For still others like the Johannine church, or the one to whom the *Epistle of the Hebrews* was addressed (unknown), it meant that the sacred symbolism of the temple was now operative on loftier planes, those of the true worship in spirit and in truth (*John*) or the more perfect tabernacle (*Hebrews*). Inevitably, Christianity was to become an increasingly gentile movement after 70 C.E., but especially in its Palestinian homeland, and possibly also among Jews of the Diaspora, the attempt was made to attract more Jews into the movement, given the spiritual upheaval and the fact that not all were attracted to the approach of the Jamnia Rabbis. Indeed, those New Testament writings that show a particular interest in Jewish practices and their reinterpretation within Christianity (e.g. *Gospels of John* and *Matthew, Epistle to the Hebrews, Epistle of James*) may well have been written with such a missionary purpose to Jews also. Inevitably, such 'proselytising' in a field that had now become extremely controversial gave rise to severe tensions, even hostility and animosity, as differing points of view, about the true meaning of the ancestral traditions were on a collision course with each other. Such expressions of hostility should never have obscured the fact that what was in dispute was the meaning of God's plan for history, which all alike accepted, but which each side interpreted in the light of their own historical experiences.

Reading *Acts* one gets little or no hint of the national struggle that was going on around the new movement and which must have touched Palestinian Christians at least, if not those in the Diaspora also. It is usual to see the so-called Apocalyptic Discourse in the Gospels (Mk 13; Mt 24-25; Lk 21) as reflecting something of the crisis of the times, especially in view of the fact that Luke (writing later) appears to have introduced explicit references to the occurrences in Judaea into his account (compare Lk 21:20-24 with Mk 13:14-20). But even in Mark's account one gets some impression of the tensions of the times. Christians in Judaea are warned to flee to the mountains, presumably to counteract the inclination to make Jerusalem their base together with the revolutionaries. Even though Christian Jews had come to believe in Jesus as the Messiah, they could easily have looked to the impending struggle with Rome as the final consummation of the age, expecting the return of Christ then. This explains the warning: 'and then if anyone says to you, "Look, here is the Christ!" or "Look, there he is!" do not believe it. False Christs and false prophets will arise and show signs and wonders, to lead astray if possible even the elect' (Mk 13:21-22). According to Josephus there were many such self-styled Messiah figures in those years and many strange signs and portents experienced, all pointing to the apocalyptic atmosphere of the times. Undoubtedly, Palestinian Christians were no more immune to these ideas than any others. Indeed their belief in Jesus might have made them even more susceptible, and that would explain the continued importance of such passages as Mt 5:38-47 (against revenge and retaliation), Mk 12:13-17 (on paying tribute to Caesar) and Rm 13:1-7 (on obedience to civil authorities), reflecting the need to warn some Christians about sharing the Zealot ideal. On the other hand there may have been a matter of coercion, for we hear of oaths by some forty zealous Jews in Jerusalem not to eat or drink until they had done away with Paul (Ac 23:12-15). In other words insofar as Christians (like other less radical Jews) were not prepared to share the ideals of the Zealots, they were in danger of being regarded as Roman collaborationists and unpatriotic.

Our historical and geographical sketch of the early Christians has necessarily been very limited, and there are many obvious lacunae. What became of Peter and the Twelve, for example? It is amazing that we know so little about this group. There is every reason to accept the fact that Peter was martyred in Rome, together with Paul. But we know nothing of how his ministry 'to the uncircumcised' (Gal 2:7) was conducted or what was its geographical extent. Our knowledge of the other members of the group is even less. Barnabas, the Jew from Cyprus who introduced Paul to the Jerusalem church and later brought him from Tarsus to Antioch must have been a very influential figure, yet beyond these few scattered references we know nothing about his ideas or achievements. Then there is the lack of any first hand information about the way that Christianity came to other great centres such as Alexandria. The likelihood is that it reached there early, since we hear of an Alexandrian Jew, Apollos, who had 'been instructed in the way of the Lord', coming to Ephesus, and eventually emerging as an influential Christian preacher, even at Corinth (Ac 18:24-28; 1 Cor 1:12; 3:6). Yet we have no information about his contribution despite the fact that he is described as 'an eloquent man, well versed in the scriptures'! Indeed we have to wait for almost one hundred years before we hear anything more about the church in Alexandria, and then we encounter a highly intellectual tradition in the persons of

Clement of Alexandria and Origen, perhaps the most creative thinker the church produced in the first three centuries. The recently discovered Coptic Gnostic library from Nag Hammadi in Egypt, though dating from the fourth century in their present form, can perhaps suggest some earlier developments among Christians in Egypt. Unfortunately we cannot as yet fill in the blanks about the origins of such trends, later to be styled heretical, and we must await the mature judgment of scholars on these documents before coming to any definitive conclusions about the church in Egypt at an earlier period.

We raise all these questions not as an incentive to useless speculation about the early Christian movement, but rather to highlight the fact that the information we do have is only *part* of the total picture. Given the limited nature of our sources and the intention of Luke in particular to give us a picture of linear development from Jesus through the Twelve to Paul, it is remarkable the degree of pluralism we have been able to detect within the movement from its very earliest days. This suggests that the total picture can only have been more diversified still – a consideration which prompts other approaches to supplement the one we have been following.

III. Who Were the Christians? Sociological Approaches

Our times have witnessed an extraordinary explosion of interest in and development of the human sciences – sociology, anthropology, psychology, for example. For many people these sciences may have something important to say about man or society, but their use in the study of religion, especially the Christian religion, is either unnecessary or inappropriate. Their insights, it is claimed, reduce Christianity to a purely human phenomenon, emptying it of all spiritual or supernatural content. While this may have been the intention of some earlier studies in these fields, it certainly need not necessarily be so, and one may legitimately ask how else can the divine or the supernatural manifest itself within this world except through the structures that are innate to man. And for his part man can only express his understanding of divine encounters in the language symbols, gestures and organisational patterns that are part of his everyday experience. Before one dismisses such 'modern' disciples then, it should be remembered that orthodox Christianity has always particularly insisted on its incarnational aspect – that is, that it exists in and through human structures, and it has resisted, at least theoretically, any temptation to abandon the human sphere. Consequently approaches which help us to understand the way we as humans behave and interact with our environment must inevitably have important insights for our understanding of the Christian movement also. Indeed there is much to be gained by asking new questions prompted by the human sciences, in view of our fragmented historical picture of early Christians. Unsuspected connections can often be detected between different pieces of isolated information, or old data can be cast in a new light, that may help us to better understand aspects of Christianity as a religion which have been neglected in the past.

One approach to the study of the early Christian movement is to discuss its initial sectarian character and to trace the process of its development into a religion, according to the descriptions of these two terms – sect and religion – in contemporary theoretical studies. A number of characteristics of a sect have been listed; it begins as a protest movement; it rejects the view of reality taken for granted by the establishment; it is egalitarian in structure and outlook; it demands total commitment from its members; and it frequently believes that an alternative social or even cosmic order will soon be established.

Put in other terms, a religious sect is not a new religion, but rather a particular emphasis within an existing one claiming that its version of the meaning of the parent religion is the only true one. On the other hand a religion is usually described as a system of beliefs, practices, rituals and structures based on a shared understanding of the meaning of the universe perceived in terms of a Supreme Being. More simply, a religion has its own distinctive understanding of the universe and its relations with the deity it worships, and this understanding determines the way in which its various structures are developed or adapted within different cultural situations.

Applying some of these categories to early Christianity one might say that the process we have been following in our historical survey was roughly the process of transforming the Jesus movement from a sect into a new and independent religion. To begin with, it is necessary to recognise that the Jesus movement can be understood both as a social and religious protest group. Insofar as we can determine the social background of Jesus' followers, it seems certain that they were from a rural and peasant ethos rather than the urban middle class. As we saw in our opening chapter this made them economically marginal people, given the overall land ownership policies that were operative in Palestine as elsewhere in the Roman world for centuries. Admittedly we do find an occasional person of the upper class in his retinue, such as Joanna, the wife of Chuza, Herod's steward (Lk 8:1-13), but this is as much a sign of the egalitarian attitudes he espoused ('neither male nor female' as Paul later puts it), as it is an indication of the level of social class of the vast majority of his followers. This does not necessarily mean that the movement was originally made up only of the down and outs of Palestinian society, since in the ancient world, much more so than in our society, class is not a matter of possessions and wealth but rather of birth and heritage. There is no reason to suspect that the sons of Zebedee, for example, were impoverished people, employed as they were in the family fish industry that could afford hired scrvants (Mk 1:20). However, as Galileans, they had been made to feel outsiders in Jewish society, despite their continued loyalty to the ancestral religion. The Scribes from Jerusalem who had visited the province on an occasional basis had not received a very welcoming reception, and they for their part were not overly impressed with the attitudes of the natives. To Johanan ben Zakkai, the re-organiser of Judaism after the destruction of the temple, is attributed the saying: 'Galilee, you hatest the Torah. Your end shall be destruction'. Another Galilean holy man, Hanina ben Dosa, though never having gathered a retinue of permanent followers like his near contemporary, Jesus of Nazareth, nevertheless showed a similar attitude of independence. It is no surprise then that the Jesus movement consciously rejected the organisational authority structures which were current within Palestinian religious and saecular life – his followers are to be the least of all and servants if they wish to be first; they should not seek honorific titles or salutations as recognised spiritual leaders (Mk 9:35; Mt 23:6-12), nor are they to lord it over others as the civil authorities do. As a Galilean protest movement both Jesus and his first followers showed an extraordinary detachment from the established signs of acceptability and divine blessing in Palestinian life – wealth, possessions and family – and pursued a lifestyle of protest *within* the society, not opting out of it like the Essenes.

Even when the movement transferred its sphere of activity beyond the borders of Palestine and in the process became largely urban-based, it did not lose its protest character entirely. Again it is not so much a question of its appeal for the genuinely impoverished, though it certainly did attract these also, but rather that people entered the new movement who did not enjoy high social rank in the Graeco-Roman world, as the sixth citation above indicates. We have suggested that the Hellenists were a very influential group in this development, and in evaluating their contribution it is important to keep in mind the protest character of their presence in Jerusalem in the first place. Presumably they had abandoned the economic and other benefits of the Diaspora in search of a more authentic Judaism, only to be disillusioned with what they found, and in the process some had chosen the Jesus movement as the most genuine option available.

This brings us to the religious sectarianism of the movement. As we have previously pointed out Jesus spoke in the name of the God of the Fathers, whose will was expressed particularly in the Hebrew Scriptures which all Jews shared in common. They differed however on the question of the definitive interpretation of those Scriptures and together with the other issues involved, differences on this question undoubtedly determined the sectarian character of first century Judaism as a whole. In other words each group claimed the Scriptures as their own, or at least that they, and they alone had the authentic means of determining their true meaning. While Jesus appears to have appealed to his own authority as much as to that of Scripture ('But *I* say to you'), it is noteworthy that the first preachers approached their task determined to show that Moses, the prophets and the psalms (i.e. the Hebrew Scriptures) had spoken of Jesus and found their fulfillment in him (cf. Ac 2:17-28; 3:17-25; 7:2-50; 10:43; Mt passim; Jn 5:39.46; Lk 24:25.44). This insight is carried further by the authors of the Pastorals who claim that the Old Testament can only lead to salvation when read through Christ (2 Tim 3:14-17). The Pharisees had claimed equal authority for their oral law and the Qumran Essenes believed that the teacher of righteousness would be the definitive interpreter of the prophets for the members of the community, each thereby affirming their claims to be the sole authentic voice of Judaism. The Jesus movement made its own of the Greek translation of the Hebrew Scripture, the Septuagint, once it had moved to the larger hellenistic world, eventually necessitating new translations for Diaspora Jews, even though the Septuagint had served them for centuries. Perhaps nothing illustrates better than this the way in which the question of Scripture stood at the centre of sectarian polemics and eventually·became the dividing wall between the two religions.

Much more could be said about the sectarian character of early Christianity, always bearing in mind that as used in this context the word does not carry the pejorative connotations that are often associated with it in today's usage. However, the application of the sect concept has helped to define the relationship between Christianity and Judaism in a new light. The obvious question now is, at what point did Christianity cease to be a movement within Judaism and begin to be an independent religion in its own right? It is at this point that a second model, drawn from the field of social anthropology, that of the 'millennial movement', can be useful in helping to understand the transformation that took place. By millennium in this context is not meant the thousand year reign of the saints (Ap 20:4-5) but rather the expectation of any group for a new order of reality, soon to be inaugurated. As already mentioned, a sect usually believes in the soon arrival of a new social and even cosmic order and so is millennarist in character. This aspect of the Jesus movement is easily documented from the apocalyptic beliefs of both Jesus and the early Christians, including Paul. Their belief in Jesus the Messiah only heightened their expectation for the soon consummation of the age with his return (Ac 3:17-21; 1 Thess 4:13-17). In such an atmosphere of heightened expectation there is little room for some of the more usual organisational aspects that we

associate with a fully developed religion. Since it is believed and hoped that the myth might soon be actual-
ised, there is not the same stress on ritual as a way of
experiencing its saving power; neither is there the same
necessity for organisational structures and the formulation of beliefs. However, once it emerges that the longed-
for consummation is not going to happen as speedily as
anticipated, a crisis emerges. Either the group abandons
its apocalyptic beliefs, and usually is disbanded altogether, or alternatively compensates for the non-event in
other ways. In the language of the cultural anthropolo-
gists the cognitive dissonance between expectation and
fact in millennial movements is overcome by other com-
pensatory factors.

The delay in the Parousia, or Second Coming of Jesus,
has for long been recognised as having been an important
factor in the development of early Christian theology.
Luke, for example, is said to have written his second
volume, *Acts of the Apostles*, to show that the present
of the church, now protracted indefinitely, was a meaningful
time in God's messianic plan for his people. Scholars have
also underlined the so-called 'realised eschatology' of the
Fourth Gospel, which no longer speaks of the future hopes
in apocalyptic and cosmic fashion but rather sees them
already realised in the community's life of love and communion with one another and with Christ, the true vine.
While these insights into the development of early Christian
theology are valid, consideration of the impact of the delay
on early Christian life and organisation would also bear
fruitful analysis in the light of the foregoing anthropological
considerations. There are at least three areas of development
that could well be further clarified by the theory of cognitive
dissonance just mentioned – ritual, mission and organisation – deserving at least a minimum treatment here.

In our opening chapter we discussed the role of initiation,
ritual and myth in the mystery religions and suggested

some similar patterns with early Christians, without necessarily arguing for a direct influence of the former on the latter. Presumably the earliest Christians had an initiatory rite, baptism, which was probably modeled on the rite of initiating proselytes into Judaism, but as demanded in *Acts* they do not seem to have any developed theological understanding of its function and purpose. It is only with Paul that we find this taking place, and then significantly, for a gentile audience, the Romans, who are reminded of the instruction they had received at their initiation (Rm 6:3-4). It was no longer simply a rite done 'in the name of Jesus' (Ac 2:38; 10:48) but rather it embodied the very act of dying and rising with Christ which was the saving myth preached by the Christians (1 Cor 15:3-6). In other words Baptism was no longer seen as a preparatory rite for the coming new age, but as a way of sharing in the redemptive power of the myth within the present. One can similarly detect a shift of emphasis in the celebration of the eucharist. In all probability the earliest expression for the distinctive memorial meal of the early Christians was 'the breaking of bread' (Ac 2:46), which recalls directly the action of Jesus at his final meal with them within the Jewish context of Passover celebration. Paul describes the eucharist as a *proclaiming* of the Lord's death until he comes (1 Cor 11:26), thus suggesting the anticipatory experience of the future consummation. While this understanding is retained subsequently (cf. for example Lk 22:28-30 – 'eating and drinking at my table in my kingdom'), by the end of the first century one detects a change of emphasis such as is reflected in the last citation for this chapter which is taken from the Roman writer Pliny. At their assemblies Christians 'sing hymns to Christ as to a God', we are told, thus suggesting that the developing Christology of the church had made a distinct impact on its liturgical life. Ritual was now seen more as a way of sharing in the life of the God-man than as a way of anticipating the coming age. It seems possible then to trace in broad lines a greater emphasis being given to

Christian ritual that corresponded with the growing awareness by the community of its own identity, outside and
independently of Judaism. At the same time it reflected
the way in which the Jewish myth of the coming new age
was gradually adapted to the realisation that it had already
been realised in the life, death and resurrection of the
Messiah Jesus.

Turning next to the missionary activity of the church, we
have seen how the Hellenists played a vital part in the beginnings of the Christian mission, after having been dispersed from Jerusalem following the death of Stephen.
While there is evidence of active Jewish proselytism in the
first century, the predominant apocalyptic view was that
the gentiles would be introduced into the coming age by an
act of God's graciousness once the true Israel had been
constituted (cf. Is 2:2-5; 60:1ff; Zech 14:16; Mt 8:11). Thus
the first Christians felt obliged to address fellow Jews
rather than engage in active mission to the gentiles. Once
again the non-event of the apocalyptic hope created a
situation of serious dissonance for the Jesus movement
that was now faced with the question of whether or not they
should abandon their beliefs and the hope for the gentiles
that went with them. Anthropological studies suggest that
rather than abandon firmly held convictions, groups attempt
to compensate by having as many as possible join the
movement, on the assumption that the more people who
join the more likely it is to be true. In this way basic doubts
are dispelled, and in the case of the early church the success
of such activity would have the added benefit of suggesting
that God's plan was still intact and being realised in another
way. Thus we find Luke speaking of the prolonged interim
as 'the times of the gentiles which must be fulfilled' (Lk
21:24) and Paul turns the Jewish apocalyptic idea upside
down by saying that once the gentiles have entered the
movement in their full quota, God will graft the Jewish
nation back onto the original root (Rm 12:11-29). Furthermore, the success of the missionary activity can silence those

who scoff at Christian credulity about the Lord's second coming. That such ridicule was encountered, presumably from Jewish circles in particular, is evidenced in one of the later documents of the New Testament, probably dating from the end of the first or early in the second century C.E. (cf. 2 Peter 3:3-9).

Finally, there is the question of community organisation. We have noted how during his lifetime Jesus appears to have consciously rejected the authority patterns that were current in both the religious and civil society of his day. Furthermore, we observed that the apocalyptic hope of the first believers made the community relatively unstructured initially, despite the presence of certain key figures such as Peter and the Twelve, whose position was based on their personal relationship with Jesus – James, whose holiness and possibly his blood relationship with the Lord gave him a position of preeminence among Jewish Christians, and Paul, who had encountered the Risen Lord. What is significant about the earliest phase of the community's life is the absence of any duly constituted offices, and authority resides in those whose life or experience can command it. Besides those mentioned this can also be illustrated by the influence of such important figures as Stephen, Barnabas and Apollos, to mention only those whose names are known to us, and who do not appear to have occupied any positions other than those acquired by personal gifts, and so were not transferable. In millennarian movements such charismatic leaders (using the word 'charismatic' in its original sense of 'gifted', but not excluding spiritual gifts) achieve their position insofar as they embody in their own persons, the ideals of the group, but the problem emerges when they themselves die or the original vision of the group is not realised. It is at this stage that the community's style of leadership together with its character must inevitably change. The words and deeds of the original charismatic leaders now become part of the community tradition that will shape and determine its future life and direction. At the same time, and of necessity, a new type of leadership emerges, whose task is not to continue the original charismatic style, thereby giving rise to the possibility of a totally new movement, but to preserve and define the community's tradition and ensure its faithful observance.

As applied to early Christianity this development has often been judged to be a serious decline, whereby the free gift of the Spirit was controlled, if not stifled, by office-holders whose positions are obtained by appointment not by personal gift. Put in these terms, the tension between the charismatic individual and the officeholder is too sharply focused, at least as such institutions as bishops and pres-byters emerged in the early church and are reflected in the later writings of the New Testament. Besides, it neglects the changed character of the community from that of apocalyptic sect to Christian church with ever increasing numbers and widening geographical extension. When one looks at the qualities demanded of the officeholders (cf. for example, 1 Tm 3:1-13; 2 Tm 1:6f; Tit 1:5-11) they clearly indicate that only people of substance will be ap-pointed to office, sober, upright and above all faithful, as behooves those whose role is defined in terms of guardian of the tradition. At the same time a number of counter-movements ensured that the consolidation of the com-munity did not exclude the charismatic entirely. In such early Christian writings as the *Third Epistle of John*, the *Teaching of the Twelve Apostles* and the letters of Clement of Rome we hear of wandering Christian preachers, who are not officeholders and who are often looked upon un-favourably by the local church authorities, precisely because they represent an independent and different form of leadership. Furthermore, as the traditions emanating from the original charismatic figures are put into writing (the Gospels and the Pauline letters) and become canonical, that is, officially recognised documents of the whole community, they keep alive the charismatic insights of those founding figures that serve as a fully legitimated criterion for criticising all subsequent leadership. It is little wonder that the Scripture has often been at the centre of controversy in the church of subsequent ages, including our own, since it contains within it the explosive dynamism to challenge all human authority in the name of the Originator of the Christian movement and those who first shared his charismatic vision.

So far we have been considering the contribution of the human sciences to a better understanding of early Christianity by focusing on its internal development from sect to new religion with its own ritual, mission and organisation. However, they can also help us in understanding the new movement's interaction with the larger Graeco-Roman ethos. The relationship is a two-way one, since as a protest movement Christianity was not merely the confluence of certain political, social and economic factors operative in the larger society, but in turn had its own impact on those very factors, because of its independent religious vision, to which it remained essentially true, despite changing circumstances. Clearly these factors and functions, as the two-sided relationship is technically described, vary from the Palestinian to the Diaspora context of the movement and for different stages of its development.

As a protest movement of renewal within Judaism, Christianity was largely a failure and had little impact on changing the patterns of Palestinian social and political relations. Throughout the first century the dominant mood there was that of a religiously militant nationalism, the direct result of Rome's mismanagement of the social and political situation it had itself created in dismantling the Jewish state at the time of Pompey. The Jesus movement was a deliberate attempt to create an alternative human community based on love instead of violence. Even though Jesus had been put to death officially by the Romans, probably because they wrongly identified him with the nationalist political threat, his followers did not abandon his gospel of love and peace for the sword, but instead made the cross the central symbol of their movement, and a sign of his and their refusal to engage in a struggle for power. Indeed, one suspects that it was this refusal to align themselves with the current dominant trend that led to the deaths of James the son of Zebedee 'to please the Jews' (Ac 12:3), and later James, the brother of the Lord, as well as the persecution of other influential leaders like Peter, John and Paul. There might have been some opportunity for Christianity in the post-70 C.E. situation to have had a real impact on Palestinian life, but by that time the movement had been dispersed in Palestine itself and its largely gentile character had given it a totally different orientation. Thus we have the ironic situation that a movement, which in terms of sociological theory was the direct product of various factors within the Palestinian milieu, failed, only to become a powerful force in the larger society that had brought about the Palestinian situation in the first place.

On the basis of our historical reconstruction Christianity came to the Diaspora through the medium of the Hellenists, Paul included, and it eventually reached the pagan world as a particular version of Diaspora Judaism. Clearly there were many factors at work in this development, some of them, such as language, universalist authors in philosophy, religion and politics, dating from shortly after Alexander's conquests. Indeed it could reasonably be argued that the Hellenists' own background in this culture made them rather than the original Twelve, the ideal spokesmen for the new movement, since they lacked the isolationist attitudes that a Palestinian Jewish background inevitably fostered – something graphically portrayed in the incident of Peter at Antioch (Gal 2:12f). Initially the identification with Judaism may not always have served the new movement's best interests, in that it became the object of anti-Jewish propaganda and slander, and perhaps this may have quickly led it to a clearer self-definition over against the parent religion. Yet not even the active persecution under Nero in which Christians were made the scapegoats for the Emperor's whims could change the basic character of the movement, but rather convinced it that it was following the pattern which the master had set. He too had been 'the scapegoat' of a Jewish aristocracy and a Roman procurator who were essentially distrustful of each other and wanted to test one another on a trumped-up charge about loyalty to Caesar. Far from destroying the movement then, persecution by the civil authorities merely consolidated its basic beliefs and attitude over against the Roman power, something that the pagan authorities could never understand.

Once Christianity moved into the Diaspora situation it became a religion of the cities, only gradually finding its way back to the villages again at the end of the first century, as Pliny's letter suggests. Inevitably this meant a change in its original form of a protest movement of Palestinian origin and intention. Nevertheless, the transfer did not mean that the basic insights were lost, or that it became totally immersed in the new culture. Rather, in the form of the house church it soon emerged as a powerful antidote to the worst features of that culture – those of displacement, uprootedness, and a rigidly authoritarian class structure, that made an easy identification of weak with poor, and strong with the well-to-do or those of noble birth, as the sixth citation at the beginning of the chapter suggests. In all probability the house churches that we hear of in Paul's letters and in *Acts of the Apostles* (Ac 16:15.31; 17:6; 18:1-8; Rm 16:3ff; 1 Cor 1:14-16; 16:19; Philem 2) were located in homes that belonged to the well-to-do, and on occasion the cultural and social differences between them and those of lower rank who had come into the new movement reasserted themselves. This is clearly one of the problems that was causing tension in the Corinthian community, and Paul's words to the 'strong' makes it quite clear that their conduct is unacceptable and their attitude a direct negation of the word of the cross, which he had made the central idea of his proclamation to them.In general however, the house churches offered a radically different community alternative for Graeco-Roman men and women, even if they might appear to outsiders to be similar to the various free associations, or *collegia* as they were called, that were an established part of the contemporary social life. Statements like, 'there is neither Jew nor Greek, slave nor free, male nor female' (Gal 3:28) were no empty slogans even long after Paul's death, as Pliny's enquiry from two female slaves who were deaconesses in the movement eloquently demonstrates. Hospitality became a particularly highly valued virtue among Christians, being a concrete expression of the love command (Rm 13:9-13; 1 Pet 4:8-10), as a network of quasi-familial relationships was established from city to city within the empire, and Christians were assured a warm welcome by their fellows on their travels, either for missionary or personal reasons, and were provided with the necessities for their journey as they left: Ac 21:4f; Philem 22; Tit 3:13f; Rm 15:23f; 1 Cor 16:11; 3 Jn. It was this practical philanthropy and sense of brotherhood rather than the depth of their philosophical analysis that struck non-believers most about the Christians, even in the second century. No doubt these traits made it particularly attractive to the lower middle classes, whose sense of alienation in the early Empire was very real. The aristocracy on the one hand and the slaves and freedmen on the other were less open to religious change, for very different reasons. And while Christianity could boast of some people of noble birth as its first members, it was not until later that the upper classes showed any great interest in the movement.

Earlier in talking about the religious developments of the times we mentioned the trend towards monotheism as a dominant feature. It was amazing then that Diaspora Judaism had not made a deeper impact on the religious consciousness of the Graeco-Roman man. There were of course full converts, the proselytes, and others who were attracted to some aspects, the God-fearers, but it was only under the impulse of Christianity that Jewish monotheism really came to be widely diffused. One can only surmise that previously other aspects of Judaism had deterred the masses from joining. Under the Christian aegis however, these aspects of Judaism which were less appealing for the common man were not required, and so the new movement was able to cash in on the monotheistic trend of the times in a way that the parent religion was not. This doctrine of God as Father of all was implicit in Jesus' attitudes towards all with whom he had come in contact within the Palestinian milieu, but it was Paul who articulated it explicitly in his doctrine of Christian freedom for the gentiles and made it the centre of his missionising programme. In doing so he gave a direction to Christianity that was ultimately to make it the religion of the Empire. But at this point we have already passed from sociology to theology.

IV. Who were the Christians?
Theological Approaches

In the previous section our primary focus was an attempt to understand the development and spread of Christianity as a sociological and cultural phenomenon, or at least to raise the question how far attention to such aspects of the movement might shed light on the incomplete historical account to which our sources restrict us. In this final section we turn our attention to a consideration of the theological development of the movement, for the shift from sect to new religion necessarily involved a system of beliefs formulated to meet the community's developing situation and to define its attitude on various issues that emerged as central to its life. Understood in this way it is clear that there is no one theological approach within the early Christian movement, and hence no one New Testament theology. While we cannot hope to cover here all the divergent points of view, it should still be a useful exercise in defining who the early Christians were to ask our sources two rather basic questions that any Graeco-Roman convert might have asked: 1) Who is Jesus Christ, and 2) What does membership in this movement have to offer in relation to the uncertainty of the times? As we shall see the answers to these questions are closely related, since unlike later Christological reflection, the first Christians never thought about Christ's person without also considering his achievement for mankind.

(i) WHO IS JESUS CHRIST?

We have already spoken of the question of the historical Jesus and the way in which the memory of him was central to the faith-life of the early Church. The earliest reflections of his person were closely related to that memory, and a number of these are still recoverable from the New Testament text. In Ac 3:17-21 Peter declares that Jesus is God's Christ (not a proper name yet, but the Greek translation of the Hebrew messiah, 'the anointed one'), who is awaiting the final conversion of Israel before he returns to inaugurate 'the restoration of all things', that is, God's new age. In this formulation the emphasis is clearly on the future work of Jesus, rather than on his past activity or his present status, though of course these are not excluded. Very closely related to this understanding is that of Peter's Pentecost speech as reported at Ac 2:36, but, as befits the occasion, the stress is rather on the reversal of fortune that Jesus has experienced at the hand of God in the resurrection: 'Let all the house of Israel know that this Jesus whom you crucified, God has made both Lord and Christ'. Here there is the addition of a second title 'Lord' which was to become very important in the Greek-speaking world because of its honorific meaning as applied to the Emperor – Lord Caesar. Perhaps then, there was a polemical edge to Luke's adding it to the other title 'Christ', given the universal audience of people from all the known quarters that he conjures up for this opening address of Peter. However, there is much older evidence that this title was applied to Jesus at a very early stage by the Aramaic-speaking Palestinian church, in an invocation that even the Greek churches had learned to pray – Maranatha, Come Lord Jesus (or 'You are Lord Jesus', 1 Cor 16:22; Rev 22:20). It is significant that it is in the liturgical celebration that we can detect the beginnings of attribution to Jesus of a status equal to God – the law of worship becomes the law of belief, as an old theological adage puts it.

However much the earliest Christians focused on the present Lordship or the soon return of Christ, inevitably the death of Jesus was a fact too engraven on their memories to be ignored or passed over. The persecution of the just man and his subsequent vindication by God was one model they could have drawn on from contemporary Judaism, but their belief in Jesus as God's Messiah inevitably pushed them to discover in this event even deeper meaning in terms of God's *mysterion* or plan for his world. One section of the Old Testament, Is 40-55, dating from the Babylonian captivity and reflecting an experience of Israel similar to their own in terms of destruction and renewal, seems to have played an important role in shaping their thinking. In particular the figure of the suffering servant as depicted in Is 53 provided the theological framework within which it was possible to see the death of Jesus as God-willed and meaningful – he died *for* our sins, just as the servant was depicted by the prophet 'carrying the sins of the many' in his suffering, only to be raised up and exalted by God (Is 52:13; 53:4f.12). This language comes in part at least from the cultic sphere of Israel's life; and so the way was clear for understanding Jesus' death as the atoning sacrifice that reconciled men with God, and it finds expression in the earliest understanding of the eucharist as the memorial meal of Christ's death until he comes (1 Cor 11:23-25; Mk 14:22-25). The *Epistle to the Romans* (cf. 3:21-31) is one place where this idea is developed, and it reaches its climax in the *Epistle to the Hebrews*, with its elaborate typology based on the ritual of the Day of Atonement (Lev 16). Yet these fuller theological treatments are only the natural development of ideas that were already part of Christian tradition when Paul entered the new movement. He tells the Corinthians that he *handed* on to them what he had *received*, that Christ died *for* our sins, *in accordance with the Scriptures*, and then goes on to catalogue those to whom the Risen Lord appeared (1 Cor 15:3-8). As we saw already, the Scriptures were the common possession of all the different Jewish groups, and each claimed their interpretation and application as definitive, so it is not a matter of an Old Testament prophet having accurately predicted the details of Jesus' career, as many simplistic discussions in the past have suggested. Rather, the Old Testament Scriptures provided the earliest Christians with the raw materials in terms of language and models for expressing their interpretation of Jesus' life and death in ideas that were consistent with their belief in the one God who had bestowed his lordship of creation on his servant Jesus (cf. 1 Cor 8:6).

The question of Jesus' relationship to God was obviously an important one, even during his lifetime, and much has been made of his use of the word *Abba* as expressive of his own intimate, personal communion with God, which he shared with his followers in the Christian prayer *par excellence*, the 'Our Father'. One expression that was easily linked with this, and would naturally have come to mind was that of Son of God, since in the Scriptures this referred to those who were especially close to God, or chosen by him for a special task like Israel (Hos 11:1) or the king (2 Sm 7:14; Ps 2), though it is not clear that the Messiah was ever actually called a son of God in Judaism of the time of Jesus. At all events, it is interesting to note the way in which the early Christians extended this title backwards in the life of Jesus, as they came to realise more fully the way in which Jesus' whole life was under the protection and election of God. In Rm 1:2-4 Paul has preserved a very old formulation that contrasts Jesus' life in the flesh with his new-found role as giver of the Spirit since his resurrection, by juxtaposing Son of David and Son of God – Jesus is Son of God in power since his resurrection from the dead. Elsewhere this same understanding of Jesus' sonship in power through the resurrection is expressed through the medium of Ps 2 (cf. v.7), a royal enthronement Psalm which sees the day of the king's enthronement as the day of his being begotten as Son of God (Ac 13:33; Heb 1:5). However, in the gospels, which were all written later than the development we are discussing – something that is easily forgotten in view of their narrative form written in the past tense – this declaration of Jesus is moved backwards to the start of the public ministry at his baptism (Mk 1:11), and eventually even to his human origins (Lk 1:32). Thus, the whole of Jesus' life is portrayed as being under the protective fatherhood of God, whose messianic Son he is now and was from the very beginning. However, this development should not be seen as though the early Palestinian Christians who first thought of Jesus as Son of God, were thinking in categories of eternal sonship, such as were developed in Trinitarian theology as the mature reflection of the later church's faith, based on the whole New Testament's understanding of Jesus. For them, Jesus' sonship referred to his human life lived in total obedience to his Father, as God's specially anointed one to bring the messianic blessings to his people.

Inevitably, however, the question of Jesus' relationship to God had to be expressed in terms other than those of being elected or anointed as God's son. In the world of Greek religious ideas there was much more room for the notion that God's power or presence could manifest itself in and through humans, whereas Jewish monotheism had stressed the otherness of God and his separateness from man. To describe somebody as Son of God could mean two very different things depending on the religious milieu in question, therefore. This very different understanding of the manner in which the divine manifests itself within the human is well illustrated by the way in which Paul and Barnabas were identified with Hermes and Zeus at Lystra (Ac 14:11-13). Even in Palestine itself such Greek conceptions had found expression at Samaria where Simon Magus had followers who saw in him 'the power of God which is called great', that is, he was acknowledged as a manifestation of God himself (Ac 8:10). While Simon is passed off as a magician of no great consequence in *Acts*, the second century Fathers of the Church, Justin, Irenaeus and Tertullien considered him to be the founder of one of the greatest threats Christianity had to face, that of Gnosticism. In all probability it was to counter this threat that the early Christians were compelled to develop other conceptions of Jesus, more directly related to those of the world in which the new movement was now taking root.

Our knowledge of Gnosticism has been enormously enhanced by the discovery of the Coptic Gnostic Library which has recently been published, since it provides first-hand documentation from Christian Gnosticism (for the most part), rather than having to rely on polemical assertions from the Church Fathers. In the light of these discoveries a growing consensus seems to be emerging that the 'heresies' (the term is at this juncture something of an anachronism) against which such New Testament writings as *1* and *2 Cor, Colossians* and the Pastoral Epistles (*1* and *2 Tim* and *Titus*) were written were of the gnostic variety, partly pagan, partly Jewish. Thus, Gnosticism is best understood as a general religio-philosophical trend that spread throughout the Graeco-Roman world in the centuries prior to Christianity, already leaving different imprints on the various existing religious movements, without itself ever having been developed into an independent sect, until Christian Gnostiscism emerged in the Second Century. Our concern here is to suggest the way in which reaction to it helped to shape other conceptions of Jesus and his work.

As the name itself implies Gnosticism has to do with *gnōsis* or knowledge, which is acquired not by philosophical speculation but through a secret revelation that is granted by the Deity to the specially chosen. By definition then Gnosticism is elitist, and one can see a certain similarity with Jewish Apocalyptic in which the hidden secrets of God are communicated to the seer. However, there is a basic difference in that the seer's task is to communicate his message to others whereas in Gnosticism the revelation is private and personal, thereby giving the individual an independence and freedom over against all external institutions. That is why authority and tradition that has been handed on in the church are so heavily stressed in the New Testament writings listed above which seek to combat gnostic influences. Besides, whereas apocalyptic has a temporal dualism in terms of the present evil age and the future good one, Gnosticism transforms this into a dualism of matter against spirit – the former is evil and the latter is the only true mode of existence. In the Gnostic view the world is not the work of a good God, and so does not reflect God's universal ordering of his creation as Stoics and Jews alike thought. Rather the material universe, man included, is the result of a falling of a portion of the divine from the sphere of light into the world of darkness where it became united with matter. *Gnōsis* gives man a proper understanding of where he is from and whither he has fallen. As the second century C.E. Christian Gnostic Theodotus puts it, *gnōsis* tells us:

> Who we were, what we became;
> Where we were, whither we were thrown;
> Whither we are hastening, from what we are redeemed;
> What birth is and what rebirth.

In these pairs of opposites we find a clear formulation of the basic contrast that exists, according to Gnosticism, between man's present condition as a corporeal being in the world, and his true origins and proper destiny freed from the shackles of this earthly existence.

Without being able to document it in detail from the sources, scholars have postulated a gnostic redeemer-myth which speaks of a pre-existent heavenly man, coming from the sphere of light and communicating the true knowledge of how the soul might transcend the various heavenly spheres that contain it as though in a dungeon within the earth and allow it to arrive at its true home with the God of Light. In achieving this mission the redeemer outwitted the 'rulers' of this world who keep man imprisoned in ignorance and are the direct antithesis of the God of Light, who is totally removed from the universe and has nothing to do with its creation or control. Clearly the Christian Gnostics could not accept the idea of Christ becoming incarnate in human flesh and sharing our common humanity with all its limitations. This gave rise to the heresy of Docetism which, as the name implies (the Greek word *dokein* means 'to appear' or 'seem'), maintained that the redeemer was not truly a man at all, but only appeared to be one in the person of Jesus. In all probability this is the heresy that was prevalent in the circles of the Johannine literature where such views are so vehemently refuted (cf. 1 Jn 3:22; 4:2). Nor could the Gnostics subscribe to the orthodox Hebraic idea of God as the creator of the universe. Indeed, Marcion, a second century Christian Gnostic, carried this to its logical conclusion by rejecting the Old Testament entirely and drastically reducing the New Testament also. It was in response to this particular challenge that the second century Roman church drew up its list of canonical or officially sanctioned books which contained the authentic Christian tradition and also included the Hebrew Scriptures as found in the Greek translation, the Septuagint (LXX).

The threat of Gnosticism to Christian beliefs can be detected even at a much earlier period however, and the 'orthodox' answer stands behind a number of new emphases in thinking about the role and person of Christ within the New Testament. Thus at 1 Cor 8:6 Christ's role in creation is affirmed in a formulaic-style passage that has clear echoes of the Jewish prayer, the *Shema*, now, however, adapted to Christian faith in Jesus. The active involvement of God in creation is transferred to Jesus, thereby ruling out any idea of matter as evil and at the same time suggesting a reason for the pre-existence of Christ other than that of being the gnostic revealer. A number of Christian hymns found in the New Testament letters develop the notion of pre-existence further (Phil 2:6-11; Col 1:15-20; cf. also 1 Pet 3:18-19.22; 1 Tm 3:16; Eph 2:14-16; Heb 1:3), apparently influenced by the figure of Wisdom, personified in the Old Testament as active with God in the work of creation (Prv 8; Ecclus 24). In particular, the hymn in *Colossians* seems to be directly addressed to gnostic speculations that underlie the whole epistle, for it presents Christ as the pre-existent one in whom the fulness (a classic gnostic term) of God resides. He has been actively engaged both in the first creation and in the new age inaugurated by his resurrection, without any suggestion that the first creation was corrupt or evil. It seems as though the author of the Epistle (either Paul or one of his disciples) has actually borrowed the language of the Gnostics to refute their ideas – not a bad rhetorical device in any age. But the end result is a deepening for the whole church of its understanding of Christ and his uniqueness over against all the other rulers and powers of gnostic cosmology.

The Gospel of John is the ultimate stage of this Christian counterattack by employing the language of the Gnostics, but formulating a quite different understanding of Jesus and his redemptive work to theirs. As already mentioned the first epistle of John appears to be attacking the docetic heresy of the apparent humanity of Jesus, and his Gospel strikes a similar note at an early stage: 'the Word became *flesh* (not 'man') and dwelt among us' (Jn 1:14). However, from its opening hymn to the *Logos* or Word that created the universe ('all things') and then entered human history full of grace and truth as the light and life of men, the Fourth Gospel, more than any other New Testament writing, has positively appropriated the language, even the dualism of the Gnostics, but without succumbing to their radical rejection of human existence in this world. Jesus is the Way, the Truth and the Life, who is from above and who will return to where he was before, in the process communicating to men the saving knowledge that leads to eternal life (Jn 6:62; 14:6; 17:3). The term Son of Man which originated in Jewish Apocalyptic (cf. Dn 7:15.23) and which is found in the Synoptics in relation to Jesus' present activity and suffering as well as to his future coming in glory, is now used to characterise his divine origins and true destiny with God (cf. Jn 1:51; 6:62). His disciples are promised the Spirit of Truth to give them full under-standing of all that Jesus has said and done (Jn 14:17; 16:13), and the life of love that they are to share with one another is merely the living out in history of the mutual love and indwelling of both Jesus and the Father that they share in because they *know* and *confess* that Jesus is the Light of the World, unlike others who are in darkness. All this is sailing very close to the wind of Gnostic ideas yet the very daring of the intellectual enterprise that is the Fourth Gospel, sum-moned up by the crisis of the times, has left us all deeply indebted to the Evangelist and his Church. Here we have the high point of New Testament reflection on Jesus, in which heavenly origins, yet real humanity are held together by a series of evocative symbols like water, light, bread, which are basic to human life in the world, yet as used by our author, constantly point beyond themselves to their 'true' meaning in the Father, who is both Light and Love (1 Jn 1:5; 4:8).

(ii) CHRISTIANITY AND SALVATION

An episode that occurred when Paul and his companion Silas were visiting Philippi during his second missionary journey aptly illustrates the significance of this topic for Graeco-Roman man. A slave girl who was also a clairvoyant, bringing considerable profit to her masters through fortune telling, followed the two Christian preachers declaiming: 'These men are servants of the Most High God; they will make known to you a way of salvation' (Ac 16:16-17). Salvation, variously understood, was on everybody's lips, and any would-be preacher or prophet had to be able to suggest some way of achieving it, to have any possibility of gaining a following. As we saw in our opening chapter the problem was symptomatic of the times – the disruption of older traditional patterns of human community had created a great sense of uneasiness about human life and its purpose, and this in turn had generated many different religious and philosophical responses, the most drastic being the one just discussed, Gnosticism. To understand the force of the Christian answer it is important to recall the pervasive influence of Fate, understood as a power that deals capriciously with and enslaves man, making human life miserable and vulnerable. The various answers to our question 'what is Christian salvation?' were fashioned in this cauldron of search, hope and despair.

The earliest answers are directly based on the Jesus movement's indebtedness to Jewish apocalyptic: Christ, as the inaugurator of the new age, saves us from the wrath to come (1 Thess 1:10), that is, from the apocalyptic trials that were expected to accompany God's final victory. Elsewhere it is stated more positively: he initiates the times of refreshment and renewal promised in the prophets (Ac 3:20f). Above all he saves from the fear of death, as the exclamation, 'Death where is your victory? Death where is your sting?' (1 Cor 15:55) so triumphantly proclaims. The rationalisations of both Stoics and Epicureans suggest that this was one of the great problems confronting contemporary man, no matter how bravely he faced it or how brazenly he tried to ignore it. The myths of the various mystery religions all dealt with the problem in some form or other, suggesting life could overcome death and achieve a more blissful beyond. As the author of the epistle to the Hebrews so poignantly puts it, men lived all their lives as slaves in fear of death (Heb 2:15). Numerous inscriptions from tombs of Jews and pagans alike show how keenly the problem of death was felt by all, no matter what their religious persuasion. It was only as the first generation began to pass on that the problem was felt acutely by Christians, and Paul has to reassure the Thessalonians for example that the dead will share equally with the living in the blessings soon to be bestowed on all who believe that God raised Jesus from the dead (1 Thess 4:13-17). As we saw in the previous chapter, it was in apocalyptic circles that Judaism first clearly formulated the belief in an after-life as a way of explaining the fate of the just who had died. As long as Christianity remained within this framework of thinking, the question of overcoming death was easily explained in relation to the community's belief that the apocalyptic hopes were fulfilled in Jesus. However, as expectation of the imminent fulfilment of apocalyptic hope began to wane, two important developments were to take place. On the one hand, belief in the survival after death of the individual was more clearly expressed in terms of an on-going relationship with the Risen Christ – never by recourse to the Greek notion of the immortality of the soul (cf. 2 Cor 5:1-10); and on the other, the presence of salvation within the here and now was more emphatically declared. We must briefly sketch the broad outlines of this latter development.

The term 'salvation' is an all-inclusive one, something of the import of which can be grasped when dealing with an ultimate category such as death. It calls for further clarification when one attempts to give it some precision for the everyday situation of man. In this regard the writings of Paul present a rich tapestry of metaphors and images drawn from various spheres of life in an attempt to spell out its meaning more fully. Some of these, such as justification, reconciliation and atonement (redemption) had particular resonance for people of Jewish background, where the sense of alienation from God because of failure to observe his covenant law was felt acutely. In the Greek world the notion of 'freedom' must have been particularly attractive in view of the constant threat of dreaded Fate, and the erosion of political freedom – the ideal of the Greek city – through the despotism, first of the hellenistic monarchies and later of Rome. Of course Paul's Jewish background undoubtedly played a role in formulation of Christian freedom, since this fundamental Israelite experience of liberation from Egypt had been kept alive and vital through the yearly celebration of Passover. Yet it is in discussing the significance of his language for pagans that one can best understand the novelty of the conception and its appeal for his contemporaries.

For Paul Christian freedom is not an assertion of a basic philosophical principle about human nature, though he certainly does not subscribe to any fatalistic view of man either. Rather, Paul locates the problem of human freedom in a mythical-historical event of the past, the sin of Adam, through which all men forfeited their glorious freedom as sons of God and became enslaved to cosmic powers, especially Sin and Death (Rm 5:12-19). Equally, its restoration is to be attributed to another historical event, the death and resurrection of Christ, which began a process that has cosmic dimensions (Rm 8:18-22). Thus the period of man's unfreedom is not eternally determined but historically limited, and from that perspective the decisive action against it is in the past. However, that does not mean that it is not possible for man once liberated to fall back again into slavery, as he so passionately asserts in the epistle to the Galatians, especially in chapter 4. Thus, while freedom has historical and cosmic dimensions it is also personal and communal. The individual has been transformed through the process of Christian initiation from slave to son, since he has now entered a new sphere of existence which Paul expresses spatially by his often-repeated phrase 'in Christ', or personally by his use of the image of 'the body (i.e. person) of Christ'. As such he enjoys the gift of sonship, sharing in Christ's experience of God as Father and does not require the protective device of the law to order his relations with God. The use of the slave/son contrast cannot fail to have very concrete content for the Graeco-Roman situation, even if one can also see its significance for Jews dating back to the Exodus. Thus Paul shows himself to be a two-culture person capable of presenting his point of view in images that are evocative for Jew and Greek alike, as he himself declares. Freedom must be carefully defined however. It does not mean libertinism on the one hand, something that Paul apparently was accused of, nor does it mean withdrawal into the inner self with a consequent rejection of life in the world of space and time that would be characteristic of a Gnostic understanding. It can be spelled out very concretely in ethical attitudes that are the fruits of the Spirit, the only true sign that we are sons and heirs: love, joy, peace, patient endurance, kindness, generosity, faith, mildness and chastity (Gal 5:13-25). Living this kind of life in the world was for Paul the real expression of Christian liberty that was grounded in the living conviction that one's life was already being lived in communion with the God who is Father of all. Such a conviction not merely takes away fear of the hereafter, it already transforms the present and the way we relate with it.

Paul's treatment of the meaning of salvation was hammered out in the hurly-burly of controversy. His opponents felt that he had been far too hasty in suggesting that the gentiles could share in the covenant promises on an equal footing with Jews who had observed the law in all its rigour. Consequently they had attempted to impose the Jewish law on his converts in Galatia as the sure guide to perfection. Paul's response was that such a rejection of God's free gift was already tantamount to falling back into slavery – a refusal to take God on his final terms as he had expressed them in Jesus. When one turns to the Fourth Gospel one seems to have entered calmer waters where there is a much more tranquil working out of the meaning of salvation. However, as we have seen, John's treatment of the person of Jesus was also developed in an aura of controversy, no less real than that of Paul, even if the problem was more subtle.

In the Fourth Gospel truth, light and life are the most characteristic expressions to define salvation, though once we do hear that 'the truth will make you *free*' (Jn 8:32). Life defined as 'life eternal', that is, 'of the age to come', is the most all-embracing of the three. While the earlier concerns about death are still operative, the notion of life which John presents is much more comprehensive. If one believes in Jesus as the resurrection and the life, one is assured of life eternal, irrespective of whether one lives or dies (Jn 11:25-26). In other words the life that Jesus offers breaks through the normal categories of biological life and death as they are experienced in the world. Present and future lose their significance in that the believer has already passed from death to life (Jn 5:24). Instead of addressing the issue in the accepted terms John transforms the question and the questioner by introducing a deeper and richer notion of life than could ever have been anticipated in the earlier categories. Light and truth become corollaries of life in that they both express the character of Jesus' work, 'the light of the world' and 'the way, the truth, the life' (Jn 8:12; 14:6), *and* at the same time, describe the condition of believers who are called to do the truth and be children of the light on the basis of their having come to Jesus (3:21; 12:36). Thus their status as Christians becomes the expression of their ethical responsibility in the world and this in turn is the pledge of their union with Christ.

As in the case of Paul's notion of freedom, the Johannine categories also appealed to the basic concerns of the religious man of the times, conceived in the broadest possible way. The uncertainty of the age and the sense of pessimism about the human condition were effectively countered by the presentation of Jesus as the true revelation of God in human history. While the experience of the Johannine community in regard to the world might appear to be a negative one on the basis of Jn 17 (cf. especially vv. 9-19), nevertheless the description of Christ as the light of the world, and the opening statement that 'all things were made through him' does not call for negative or isolationist behaviour. No matter how much the contrasts of light and darkness, truth and falsehood, life and death appear to suggest a rejection of outsiders, the fact remains that by his being lifted up Jesus draws all men to himself (Jn 12:32), a belief that is graphically symbolised in the three languages on the cross (Jn 19:20). A community with such a vision of the meaning of its founder's life could never despise the world for whose life he had given his in love (Jn 3:16).

Conclusion: Rome and the Christians

We have attempted to trace the emergence of early Christianity from Jewish sect to new religion along historical, sociological and theological lines. As a way of testing this development at least in its broad outlines, it is useful to recall the way in which Christians were perceived by the outsiders, or more specifically by the Roman authority in the first and early second centuries. We saw in the last chapter that initially little distinction was made between the new movement and the parent religion. Claudius' expulsion of the Jews from Rome would appear to have included Christians also. And though Christians suffered at the hands of Nero, it is important to realise that there was as yet no official Roman policy about the movement. Even the persecution of Christians under Domitian, reflected in the *Apocalypse* of John, should be seen in the same light, and as part of a general reign of terror against all kinds of threats, real or imagined, that marked the latter part of his reign. Christians were certainly not very popular, it would seem, in the first century. They were accused of standoff-ishness, atheism (that is, rejection of the Roman gods) and all kinds of criminal offences, so that they could be made the whipping boy of an individual emperor's or a local magistrate's whim without arousing too much outrage from the populace at large (*1 Peter*; letters of Clement of Rome for example). However, the *Apocalypse* suggests the emergence of a more serious problem, Emperor worship: 'All who dwell on earth will worship it (the Beast, that is the Roman Emperor), every one whose name has not been written in the book of life' (Apoc 13:8). The fact that the Jews were allowed to worship their own God, rather than participate in the religion of the Empire, was seen as a concession to an ancient people and for ethnic reasons, but Christians could claim immunity from worship on no such grounds. Their refusal to worship the Emperor in particular could easily be construed as seditious, since the Emperor cult was as much a civil as a religious act that did not exclude membership in some other religious group. Why then did Christians so stubbornly reject the idea?

Julius Caesar was the first Roman to have divine status conferred on him by the Roman Senate after his assassination in 42 B.C.E., and apparently this set a pattern for later emperors. However, the tendency was to extend this status to his earthly life, especially in the East, where the notion of the divine origins of the ruler had ancient roots. There is the example of the Emperor Claudius firmly prohibiting the Alexandrians from setting up a cult to himself, 'since I do not wish to be offensive to my contemporaries, and my opinion is that temples and such forms of honour have by all ages been granted as a prerogative of the gods alone'. However, not all his successors showed the same restraint and by the time of Diocletian in the third century the idea of the God-ruler was well established. It provided a focal point for the loyalty of the citizens and the unity of the empire, and so could be used against subversive groups like the Christians. Thus in Pliny's letter to Trajan, (part of) which forms citation eight for this chapter, we see the governor demanding that believers recant their crime of being Christian by worshipping the emperor, and refusal to do so was a clear indication of their guilt and legitimate grounds for their being punished. Christ worship and Emperor worship were, even in Roman eyes, mutually exclusive, and on this understanding a more stringent policy in regard to Christians had been developed. The emperor, in his reply to the governor, confirms the legality of his actions, yet at the same time insisted that Christians should not be ferreted out or anonymously condemned. As always, Roman pragmatism had taken a middle position, yet a pattern was set that was subsequently continued by others, as Christians lived a precarious legal situation of practical tolerance, combined with official condemnation that could and did erupt against them in bitter persecution of a more systematic kind.

Given this deep-seated tension between Roman imperial policy and the Christian faith, it is natural to ask, how it is that Christianity not merely survived but actually became the official religion of the empire within three centuries? Many different answers to that question have been proposed, and no doubt the reasons are complex and diverse. Just a few of the more important ones may be suggested here that relate to the view of early Christianity and its relationship with its world that we have been suggesting. While the new religion had many aspects in common with the mystery religions, the essential difference between them was that the Christian myth was irrevocably tied to an historical person, Jesus of Nazareth, and when this was in danger of being eroded from within in Christian Gnosticism a docetic Christ was firmly rejected. Thus while sharing in the appealing aspects of the mystery religions, Christianity scored highly in terms of its concrete, historical aspect that located the saving event within this world and not in some nebulous beyond. At the same time it developed a philosophical current that was eclectic from the start, yet was able ɪo incorporate Stoic and Cynic moral ideals about the good life with the ritual and mythic elements of the religion proper. From Diaspora Judaism it inherited the idea of a universal mission to all humankind, but in breaking with the parent religion it was able to leave behind its ethnic particularism. Perhaps nothing was more important in terms of its later success than the fact that as a result of this break it was able to combine a cultural pluralism with a common faith shared by all, even when the varying expressions of that faith were themselves reflections of the diverse cultures in which the movement was at home. While Christians were allegedly subversive and anti-social, in fact the opposite proved to be the case; and this in time came to be recognised by the Roman state also, so that Constantine's act of official recognition of the Christian religion in the Eastern provinces in 324 C.E. was not just the result of his personal conversion, but a shrewd political judgment also. Christianity had in the end outlasted its competitors – Jewish and Pagan alike – and in the process had won for itself the official backing of the saecular power. Whether or not this alliance with political power was in the long-term interests of the new movement is still in the process of being answered. Insofar as Christians have been able to benefit from the support of the saecular power, the alliance has clearly been to its advantage in terms of numbers and extension. Unfortunately, it has not always been so clear that it has been of genuine assistance in keeping alive the radically different type of community life that its founder proposed, and that its first proponents found so effective in a Roman world desperately in need of such an alternative.

FOR FURTHER READING

1. Collections of Texts and Sources.

BARRETT, C.K., ed. *The New Testament Background, Selected Documents.* New York: Harper and Row/ Torchbooks, 1961.

    The best selection available of readings from ancient sources, Jewish, Roman and Hellenistic for New Testament students. Unfortunately, there are some important omissions.

DUNGAN, D., and D.L. Cartridge, eds. *Source Book for Comparative Study of the Gospels,* 3rd ed. Missoula, Montana: Scholars Press, 1976.

    Collection of ancient texts for literary comparison with New Testament writings. Useful supplement to Barrett.

RICE, D.G. and J.E. Staumbach, eds. *Sources for the Study of Greek Religion.* Missoula, Montana: Scholars Press, 1979.

ROBINSON, J.M., ed. *The Nag Hammadi Library in English.* New York: Harper and Row, 1977.

    Collection of all the tractates with brief introductions.

VERMES, G. *The Dead Sea Scrolls in English,* 2nd ed. Baltimore: Pelican Books, 1978.

    Texts and introductions.

2. General Works of New Testament Introduction and Related Areas.

AHARONI, I., and M. Avi Yonah, eds. *The Macmillan Bible Atlas.* New York: Macmillan, 1968.

    The best historical atlas available with detailed maps and references to ancient sources particularly valuable features.

BENKO, S., and J.J. O'Rourke, eds. *The Catacombs and the Colosseum. The Roman Empire as the Setting of Primitive Christianity.* Valley Forge, Pennsylvania: Judson Press, 1971.
A useful collection of essays on a wide range of topics from education to religion with suggestions for further study.

BLIGH, J., *H.I.N.T.S. Historical Information for New Testament Students.* London: Burns and Oates, 1967.
Brief compact presentations of relevant data with charts and tests to achieve accurate information.

LOHSE, E., ed. *The New Testament Environment.* English translation. Nashville: Abingdon Press, 1976.
Perhaps the best general introduction available covering both Judaism and the Graeco-Roman environment with emphasis on the religious issues.

REICKE, B., ed. *The New Testament Era: The World of the Bible From 500 B.C. to A.D. 100.* English translation, London: A. and C. Black, 1968.
The best historical introduction available.

SAFRAI, S., and M. Stern, eds. *Compendia Rerum Judaicarum ad Novum Testamentum. The Jewish People in the First Century.* 2 vols. Philadelphia: Fortress Press, 1974 & 1976.

SHULTZ, S., ed. *Jesus in his Time.* Philadelphia: Fortress Press, 1971.
Collection of essays of a popular nature by German scholars, yet highly informative for the general student.

CHAPTER ONE. The Greek Inheritance.

BULTMANN, R., ed. *Primitive Christianity in its Contemporary Setting.* English translation. New York: Meridian Books, 1956.
Especially good on classical Greek religion and Hellenistic syncretism.

CUMONT, F., ed. *Astrology and Religion Among the Greeks and Romans.* New York: Dover, 1960.
An older study of an important topic, still valuable.

DODDS, E.R., ed. *The Greeks and the Irrational.* Berkeley: University of California Press, 1951.

An important study of the non-rational primitive forms of Greek religion.

FERGUSON, J., ed. *The Heritage of Hellenism.* London: Thames and Hudson, 1973.

An excellent popular study of the Hellenistic world as a companion to P. Brown's classic on the later Roman Empire.

HENGEL, M., ed. *Judaism and Hellenism.* 2 vols. Philadelphia: Fortress Press, 1974.

Definitely for the more advanced student, but a classic on the question of the impact of Hellenism on the Jewish faith and practice before the Christian era.

NILSSON, M., ed. *A History of Greek Religion.* New York: Norton, 1964. *Greek Piety.* New York: Norton, 1964.

The former deals with the classical forms of Greek religion and the later with more popular expressions by a recognized authority in the field.

NOCK, A.D., ed. *Conversion. The New and the Old in Religion from Alexander the Great to Augustine of Hippo.* New York: Oxford Paperbacks, 1961.

Excellent discussion of the development and impact of the mystery religions.

TARN, W. and G. Griffith. *Hellenistic Civilisation.* London: Arnold, 1952.

An excellent general introduction to the many different aspects of Hellenism, including the religious and philosophical.

CHAPTER TWO. The Roman World.

BROWN, P., ed. *The World of Late Antiquity. From Marcus Aurelius to Mohammad.* London: Thames and Hudson, 1971.

A brilliant study of the later Roman Empire and its influence on the spread of Christianity.

CUMONT, F., ed. *Oriental Religions in Roman Paganism*. New York: Dover, 1950.
>   An important complement to Nock's study of the Mystery Religions in the Roman World.

GRANT, F.C., ed. *Ancient Roman Religion*. Indianapolis: Bobbs- Merrill Co., 1957.
>   Useful survey of material on Roman religion with reference to the historical sources.

SHERWIN-WHITE, A.N., ed. *Roman Society and Roman Law in the New Testament*. Oxford: University Press, 1963.
>   Excellent discussion by a classicist of aspects of the gospels and *Acts* in relation to the Roman world.

CHAPTER THREE. Judaism.

BICKERMAN, E. *From Ezra to the Last of the Maccabees. The Foundations of Post-Biblical Judaism*. New York: Schocken, 1962.
>   A good popular treatment by an outstanding scholar of the development of Judaism and its interaction with the Persian and Greek worlds.

DOUGLAS, M., *Purity and Danger*. London: Routledge and Kegan Paul, 1966.
>   An anthropologist looks at the concept of purity in general and its role in Jewish life.

FREYNE, S. *Galilee from Alexander to Hadrian. A Study of Second Temple Judaism*. Wilmington: Michael Glazier, Inc./Notre Dame Press, 1980.
>   A detailed treatment of Judaism and its encounter with Hellenistic civilization in the homeland of Jesus.

NEUSNER, J. *From Politics to Piety. The Emergence of Pharisaic Judaism*. Englewood Cliffs: Prentice Hall, 1973.
>   A good discussion for the non-expert of the problems of using ancient sources for a study of Pharisaism.
>   *First Century Judaism in Crisis. Yohanan ben Zakkai and the Renaissance of Torah*. Nashville: Abingdon Press, 1973.

A popular treatment of a more detailed study of the father of rabbinic Judaism and its emergence after 70 C.E.

RHOADS, D. *Israel in Revolution 6-74 C.E. A Political History Based on the Writings of Josephus.* Philadelphia: Fortress Press, 1976.
A good discussion of the rise and impact of the Zealots in the first century C.E.

RIVKIN, E. *A Hidden Revolution. The Pharisees Search for the Kingdom Within.* Nashville: Abingdon Press, 1978.
A provocative and perceptive study of the Pharisees' contribution to Judaism, seen as a response to the Hellenistic environment.

SANDMEL, S. *Judaism and Christian Beginnings.* New York: Oxford University Press, 1978.
An excellent survey of Jewish literature and religion for the second temple period, and a perceptive look at Christian origins by a Jewish scholar.

SCHALIT, A., ed. *The World History of the Jewish People.* Jerusalem: Masada Publishing Company, 1972.
Articles by V. Tcherikover on Hellenism and its impact on Jewish life are particularly illuminating.

CHAPTER FOUR. Christians.

CHADWICK, H. *The Early Church.* Baltimore: Penguin Books, 1967.
A lucid and helpful book on the development of Christianity in the post-apostolic age to Constantine.

CONZELMANN, H. *Jesus.* Philadelphia: Fortress Press, 1961.
A discussion of the problem of the historical Jesus, and a presentation of the results.

History of Primitive Christianity. Nashville: Abingdon Press.
A presentation of early Christian history from a critical perspective on *Acts.* Some additional (to Barrett) primary material.

CROSSAN, J.D., *The Dark Interval. Towards a Theology of Story*. Chicago: Orbis Books, 1976.
A provocative introduction to Jesus as parabler drawing on contemporary insights into story as a metaphor.

DUNN, J. *Unity and Plurality in the New Testament*. Philadelphia: Westminister Press, 1977.
A comprehensive discussion of the different theological approaches within the New Testament.

GAGER, J. *Kingdom and Community. The Social World of Early Christianity*. Englewood Cliffs: Prentice-Hall, 1975.
An epoch-making book in regard to the study of early Christianity from the perspectives of sociology and anthropology.

GRANT, R.M., *Early Christianity and Society*. New York: Harper and Row, 1977.
Seven interesting studies of various aspects of early Christian life and attitudes as these developed from the apostolic to the post-apostolic age within the Empire.

HENGEL, M. *Was Jesus a Revolutionary?* Philadelphia: Fortress Press, 1974.

KECK, L. *A Future for the Historical Jesus*.Nashville: Abingdon Press, 1977.
An excellent *status quaestionis*, and guide towards a moderate position.

The New Testament Experience of Faith. St. Louis: Bethany Press.
An excellent, dense study of the development of early Christianity at various centres in Palestine and the Diaspora. Concentrates on Pauline churches.

MALHERBE, A.J., *Social Aspects of Early Christianity*. Baton Rouge: Louisiana State University Press, 1977.
An interesting and well-documented discussion of early Christian social status with special reference to levels of literacy and the house churches.

PERRIN, N., *The New Testament: An Introduction*. New York and Chicago: Harcourt, Brace, Jovanovich, 1974.
The best introduction to New Testament literature from the perspective of modern literary and redactional studies.

THEISSEN, G. *Sociology of Early Palestinian Christianity*. Philadelphia: Fortress Press, 1978.
An equally important and challenging study from a sociological perspective, contrasting the Jesus movement with others within Palestinian Judaism.

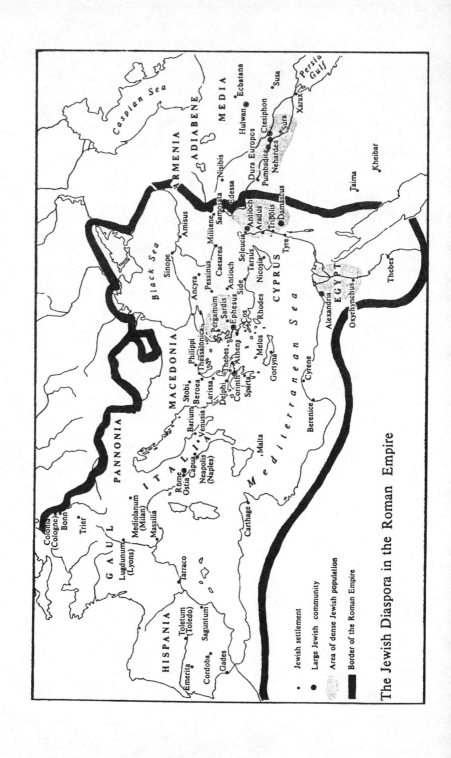

The Jewish Diaspora in the Roman Empire

- Jewish settlement
- **•** Large Jewish community
- Area of dense Jewish population
- ▬ Border of the Roman Empire

Map labels:

Caspian Sea · ARMENIA · ADIABENE · MEDIA · Ecbatana · Susa · Persian Gulf · Hulwan · Ctesiphon · Sura · Xarax · Pumbaditha · Nehardea · Taima · Kheibar · Nisibis · Edessa · Dura Europos · Samosata · Militene · Antioch · Tripolis · Damascus · Amisus · Sinope · Pessinus · Caesarea · Aradus · Ancyra · Pergamum · Seleucia · Tarsus · Tyre · Black Sea · Sardis · Ephesus · Side · CYPRUS · Cos · Rhodes · Nicosia · Philippi · Thessalonica · Beroea · Thebes · Delphi · Athens · Melos · Gortyna · EGYPT · Alexandria · Oxyrhynchus · Thebes · Stobi · Larissa · Corinth · Sparta · Mediterranean Sea · MACEDONIA · Barium · Venusia · Malta · Cyrene · Berenice · ITALY · Rome · Capua · Ostia · Neapolis (Naples) · Carthage · PANNONIA · GAUL · Mediolanum (Milan) · Massilia · Colonia (Cologne) · Bonn · Trier · Lugdunum (Lyons) · HISPANIA · Tarraco · Toletum (Toledo) · Saguntum · Emerita · Cordoba · Gades

PALESTINE in HELLENISTIC and ROMAN TIMES

- - - - Chief routes
——— Territorial, Boundaries
▲ Hellenistic Cities
▆ Roman (Herodian) Towns

ABILENE

Sidon

Damascus

PHOENICIA

Tyre

Paneas (Caesarea Phillippi)

TRACHONITIS

▲ Antiochia

▲ Seleucia

BATANAEA

Ptolemais (Accho)

GALILEE

Bethsaida (Julias)

GAULANITIS

Tiberias

▆ Hippos

▆ Dion

AURANITIS

Sepphoris

Philoteria

▆ Arbila

Dora ▲

Gaba

▲/▆ Itabyrion (Tabor)

▆ Gadara

N

Straton's Tower (Caesarea)

Scythopolis

Pella

DECAPOLIS

Samaria (Sebaste)

▆ Gerasa

SAMARIA

Shechem

Jopra

Lydda

JUDEA

PERAEA

▲ Philadelphia

Jamnia

Azotus

Jerusalem

▲ Marisa

▆ Adora

▲ Gaza

IDUMAEA

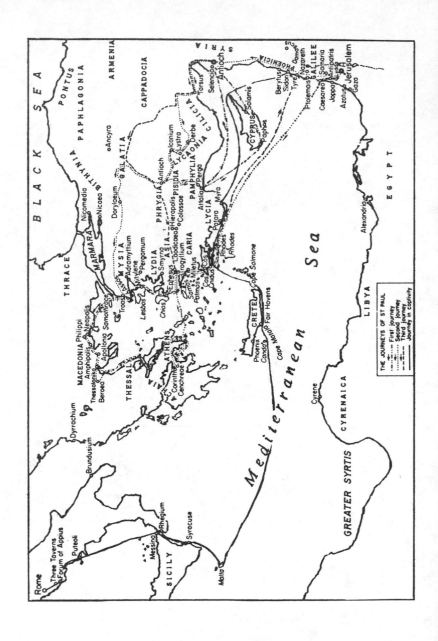